YEHUDI MEN̶ ☙ S0-ARM-038 ̶ ̶ ̶ GUIDES

Horn

Dear Lindsey,
　Congratulations on your
High school graduation!
I t has been a joy to
watch you grow up over
the 7 years that we've
worked together. I hope
that all good things will
come to you throughout your
life. I wish you joy!

　　　with deep affection
　　　Tren Cheshier
J: DD may 8th 2002

YEHUDI MENUHIN MUSIC GUIDES

Also Available
Violin and Viola by Yehudi Menuhin and William Primrose
Piano by Louis Kentner
Clarinet by Jack Brymer
Oboe by Leon Goossens and Edwin Roxburgh
Percussion by James Holland
Musicology, a practical guide by Denis Stevens
Cello by William Pleeth
Flute by James Galway
Voice edited by Sir Keith Falkner

YEHUDI MENUHIN MUSIC GUIDES

Horn

Barry Tuckwell

MACDONALD & CO
LONDON & SYDNEY

Copyright © 1983 by Barry Tuckwell

First published in Great Britain in 1983 by
Macdonald & Co (Publishers) Ltd
London & Sydney

Maxwell House
74 Worship Street
London EC2A 2EN

ISBN Cased 0 356 09096 5
     Limp 0 356 09097 3

Filmset, printed and bound in Great Britain by
Hazell Watson & Viney Ltd, Aylesbury, Bucks

Contents

Contents

Illustrations

Illustrations

Acknowledgements

I want to thank all those who assisted me with this book.
Penny Hoare and Bob Knowles from Macdonald's
editorial staff gave me endless support and
encouragement. Henry Raynor and Hugh Young in a
quite different way made me see how I should write it.
My wife Hilary and Amanda Marshall helped in
researching and organizing much of the historical data.
However, my special gratitude goes to Peter Moore who
worked so long and hard for me. Without his help I
would still be writing the book

Barry Tuckwell

The publisher wishes to thank EMI for permission to
reproduce the author's account of Giovanni Punto's life
on pp. 124–7, first printed as a sleeve note to his
recording of Punto's Horn Concertos, and the following
for permission to reproduce musical extracts: Boosey and
Hawkes Ltd., from Britten's *Serenade*; J. & W.
Chester/Edition Wilhelm Hansen London Ltd., from
Thea Musgrave's Horn Concerto; J. Curwen & Sons,
from Dame Ethel Smyth's *Double Concerto for Horn,
Voice and Orchestra*; Durand et Cie, from Dukas's
L'Apprenti Sorcier and *Villanelle*; Novello & Co., from
Richard Rodney Bennett's *Actaeon* and from Elgar's
Second Symphony; Schott & Co. Ltd., from Hindemith's
Concert Music for Brass and Strings and his Horn
Concerto, and from Stravinsky's *Firebird*; and Universal
Editions (Alfred A. Kalmus Ltd.) from Iain Hamilton's
Voyages, from Schoenberg's Wind Quartet, from
Strauss's *Don Juan*, *Don Quixote*, and *Till Eulenspiegel*,
and from Webern's *Symphonie*.

YEHUDI MENUHIN MUSIC GUIDES

Editorial Board:

General editor:	Yehudi Menuhin
Coordinating editor:	Patrick Jenkins
Advisers:	Martin Cooper
	Eric Fenby
	Robert Layton
	Denis Stevens
Drawings:	Tony Matthews
Music examples:	Malcolm Lipkin
Design:	Keith Anderson

Preface
by Yehudi Menuhin

Barry Tuckwell's wonderfully informative book about the Horn, its history, its great players, its character and demands, tempts even a violinist into strange ambitions, encouraging in him a tactile affection and sympathy for that strange metal instrument controlled not so much by the arms as by those mysterious and secretive means, somewhat damp and yet so agile, of lips, tongue and mouth. Certainly I was inspired by reading the book and could not resist applying my new insight into the ways of wind to a long Norwegian shepherd's horn, wrapped in tree bark, which appealed to me while on a cruise of the North Cape. Needless to say, I did not attempt any of those exquisite refinements of pitch and quality achieved by the gradual and sensitive introduction of the hand into the bell. It seemed inappropriate for this rustic instrument, as well as my rustic, not to say, primitive, technique – and, besides, the horn was far too extended for my short arm to attempt any manual manipulation of nuance. Nonetheless I made it speak (even if a sheep or dog hearing it would have reacted with contempt) achieving my best blast ever.

Certainly it was much better than my efforts on the *Alphorn* which I first tried with my youngest son, Jeremy, then three, when we were walking in Gstaad in the Bernese Oberland some thirty years ago. With those fantastically long mountain horns it should be remembered the player is some twenty feet removed from the bell and I let go a series of screeches with, I'm afraid, a very low signal value. But my small son, with all the easy assurance of youthful talent, produced a series of harmonics as pure as the maker of that enormous instrument intended them to be.

My only other attempt took place during the War after a late supper with Denis Brain when we returned to my hotel room at Claridges around 11 o'clock to collect his instrument and I seized the unique opportunity of learning something about the horn from the hand, one might say, from the mouth, of a master. Denis instructed, I prepared myself. When the great moment arrived, my call (or raspberry) if not attractive was at least *effective*, for not a few minutes later slow, heavy footfalls were heard down the corridor and a plaintive, pathetic male voice implored: 'All I ask for is a little peace and quiet.' We were quick to grant his request.

I returned, relieved, to the violin, leaving to the Barry Tuckwells and Denis Brains and to the readers of this excellent book the happy task of continuing the noble art of the horn. Henceforth I will play the Brahms Horn Trio with far greater understanding of my air-borne colleagues.

With gratitude to our intrepid hunting forebears and to the author, I wish this book the success it deserves.

Author's Preface
'The Horn Player Missed a Note'

'The horn', says the *Oxford Companion to Music*, 'has the reputation of possessing the most difficult technique of all the instruments of the orchestra; every regular concert-goer has experienced the shock of hearing even famous players "crack" on a note.'

This reputation is one of the most regrettable aspects of a horn player's life. Every instrument is difficult to play, and to say that the horn is more so than the others is an over-simplification. It would be more accurate to say that the horn is more treacherous than the others. This is due to many factors in its design as the contour of its tubing is different. However, the layout of the tubing, bent into a shape derived directly from the *cor de chasse*, does not affect the tone. The basic F horn is approximately twelve feet long, and the three valves add a further five feet to bring the total to around seventeen feet, making it, with the exception of the largest tubas, the longest of all brass instruments. This great length of tubing is no more than 9 millimetres in diameter at the mouthpiece, less than any other brass instrument, and the diameter of the bell is about a foot, which, except again for the tuba and some band instruments, is the largest of any of the brass. The mouthpiece is shaped like a funnel, whereas all other brass instruments have cup shaped mouthpieces.

The range of the horn extends from A-concert below the bass clef upwards for three and a half octaves, and in some baroque music as high as the B above the treble stave. Thus the horn, with its small mouthpiece and long tubing, has a range that covers all but the lowest tuba notes and the highest trumpet notes. Overriding the immense range demanded of the horn player is the fact that, acoustically, the horn is not very efficient as a means of making a sound. It could be made more efficient by redesigning the mouthpiece, giving it more of a cup shape; the tubing could be enlarged at the mouthpiece end and could incorporate more that is cylindrical, but the instrument so modified would not sound the same and it would be a cross between a trombone and a euphonium. The acoustical problem would have been alleviated to some extent, but at the price of destroying the one justification for playing the horn – its unique quality of sound. So in order to have an instrument that has a horn-like sound, the contour and layout of the tubing must remain basically inefficient.

All wind instruments are beset in one way or another by the problem of condensation, which collects at the bottom of every coil of a brass instrument's tubing, as many as fourteen on many horns. If any one of those curves occurs where there is a nodal point of the internal vibration and water has been allowed to collect there the note may be almost uncontrollable, and the player must take care that it is removed. Condensation is more of a problem in cold weather, so performances in cold concert halls or out of doors pose special problems for the horn player, since the condensation builds up more quickly.

It is all too often assumed that the valves make the horn easier to play. There are too many references to the so-called primitive natural horn as 'little more than a coiled length of tubing flared at one end, the player selecting the note he requires by changing the pressure of lips and breath,' it not being realized that the valve horn is still only a coiled length of tubing flared at one end, but now with three extra coiled lengths of tubing attached to it which can be added to the main part of the instrument by turning a valve. There are six additional sets of harmonics for the player to choose from, each harmonic selected in the same old way by changing the pressure of lips and breath. The catch is that, although the player now has all the notes of the chromatic scale at his disposal, the extra plumbing detracts from the efficiency of the instrument. When valves were first built on to the horn they were placed where it was most convenient for the manufacturer, i.e. where they could be operated conveniently by the fingers of the player's left hand. This is not necessarily the best place for them acoustically, but it is still used on instruments built today. (The Vienna horn's valves, on the other hand, are placed the other way up, that is to say, the actual valve mechanism is below the slide and the condensation goes to one central point so that it is easier to drain.) So, the horn player still has to change the pressure of lips and breath in order to select the desired note, only now he is using a less efficient tube.

No player on any instrument is note-perfect, but the horn's reputation for being difficult and consequently more liable to cause the player to miss notes is both an advantage and a curse. Most horn players will accept that their task is difficult and do not mind the general public being made aware of it, but it is annoying that so many listeners and critics wait for slips and then comment that 'the horn player missed a note', especially if it is the *only* one in the concert that was missed.

An Introduction to the Principles of Brass Playing

Brass instruments are simply lengths of metal tubing. There are many differences between types of instrument, particularly in tube length and diameter, but the sound is always produced in the same way. The player buzzes his lips into one end of the tube, thereby resonating the air contained within it.

The sounds which are produced are not random, nor are they in any way produced by singing. Only certain notes are available on a length of tubing and they follow a strict pattern. In conventional notation this pattern looks irregular, but once analysed its precise mathematical and acoustical form is clear.

This pattern of notes is called the harmonic series. Every note vibrates at a certain rate and the distance between one harmonic and the next is the same number of vibrations per second. For example, if the first note (called the fundamental) had a frequency of 100 vibrations per second, the second harmonic would have a frequency of 200 vibrations per second, and the third 300 and so on. Also, each higher octave always has double the number of vibrations per second of the octave below.

Some of the notes of the series are not in tune with the tempered scale and are not normally used, so it has become standard practice to notate them in a different way; in this case as black notes.

Horn

The number of notes in the series is infinite, but the player is limited to those within his physical capacity. The different notes are obtained by varying the tension of the lips, called the embouchure, and the pressure of air blown into the instrument. To obtain a high note the player must squeeze his lips very tightly and blow harder. To play a low note a more relaxed embouchure is required and the breath support must be less strong. Even within the human range no individual player is able to produce all the harmonics. Just as some people have high and some low voices, horn players also excel in a particular register.

Another limiting factor affecting the availability and quality of the harmonics is the length of the tube, which determines the pitch and therefore the number of harmonics within the player's reach. The average player's range is:

If a horn was built twelve feet long, the harmonics would be:

But if it was built half that length, i.e. six feet, the harmonics would be an octave higher:

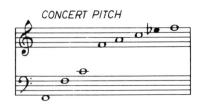

with the result that only eight as opposed to sixteen notes would be within the normal player's range.

The contour of the tubing, i.e. whether it is cylindrical and so the same shape throughout most of its length, or conical and flaring, affects the efficiency and the quality of sound. But, it should be noted that the shape into which the tube is bent has very little effect on its acoustical characteristics.

The horn is perhaps the least efficient instrument of the brass family, but it produces the most beautiful sound of all.

One
Ancestry

The horn has been called one of the oldest musical instruments, but this is not accurate. The present-day horn is a descendant of the animal horn used by primitive man. However, that was a signalling device. The horn as a musical instrument is only a few hundred years old, beginning its life in the late seventeenth century, which makes it one of the newer instruments of the baroque era.

It may never be known when it was found that a loud, penetrating sound could be made by vibrating the lips into one end of an animal horn, or even whether this occurred before or after other natural objects like bones, sea-shells or hollow logs were used in a similar fashion, but it must have been an astonishing discovery.

The short length and wide, flaring bore of an animal horn restricts the number of notes – usually one or two –

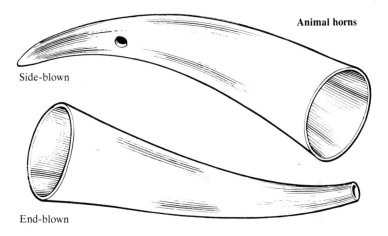

Animal horns

Side-blown

End-blown

that can be produced and in turn this limited its use to signalling for hunting and for fighting. Later it was used for military ceremonies and parades and during religious ceremonies.

Because the narrow end of an animal horn is closed, it would have been necessary to bore a hole in some way, perhaps with a hard, sharp stone or by using hot embers to burn into the horn. This hole had to be shaped into a convenient size for the lips, so that the bore actually began with an inverse cone much like the present-day mouthpiece.

The *shofar* or *keren*, the ram's horn, is blown in Jewish religious ceremonies. It was played in Biblical times and continues to be played in the same way. There are four signals or calls:

   (i) the *tqiâ*, which is a long sound on the upper note preceded by a short grace note from the lower note;
  (ii) the *švarûm*, which is a rapid alternating pattern between the two notes;
 (iii) the *trūă*, which begins on the lower note: this is played with a wide vibrato and finishes on the upper note;
  (iv) the *tqiâ gdolă*, which is the simplest of all and comprises one long sound on the upper note.

Horns and horn-like objects made from metal were used extensively in ancient times. It is known, for example, that the Jews blew on rams' horns as they marched round the walls of Jericho. Another early reference to the horn comes from the Greek historian Polybius (*c.* 204–122 BC), who related how a certain breed of pig would recognize its own horn call. In the fourteenth century BC King Tushratta offered presents to King Amenophis IV, the Pharaoh of the eighteenth dynasty, which included forty gold-covered horns, some of which were studded with precious stones. There is a relief in the British Museum from Carchemish, the ancient Hittite city on the Euphrates, dated *c.* 1250 BC, showing a short, thick horn being played, and the *si-im*, simply 'horn', is mentioned in several inscriptions of the Sumerian priest-king Gudea.

Many different types of man-made horn-like instrument have been constructed in many civilizations, but they have all had one factor in common: whatever shape they may have been bent into, the tube itself was conical, i.e. its bore increased with its length. Although they are different species of the same horn family, other metal instruments like the trumpet and trombone differ in that their tubes are cylindrical throughout most of their length, and this accounts for their more brilliant tone.

The lur

The earliest man-made horn-like instrument in Europe was the Scandinavian lur. Dating back to the beginning of the sixth century BC, the lur was still in use five centuries later. Several were preserved in peat bogs and are now housed in the National Museum in Copenhagen. They were built in mirror-image pairs and their resemblance to a set of mammoth tusks is the greatest clue to their origin. Usually measuring from two to three metres long, they are conical, ranging from about seven millimetres across at the mouthpiece to about 55 millimetres at the curiously flat bell. The mouthpiece, an integral part of the lur, was cup-shaped, rather like that of a trombone.

The surviving examples are all made of bronze in several sections and are splendid examples of the metal worker's craft of the period. However, there was one made of gold, which was stolen, presumably for the value of the metal.

The sound of the lur is very loud and rough, and although it is possible to play half a dozen notes it would be wishful thinking to imagine that it had any musical potential. The spectacular elevation of the bell would have made it ideal for the battlefield and its raucous tone has excellent carrying power and it would not seem unreasonable to suppose that the pairs of lurs were equally useful visually and aurally on the military parade ground.

Horn

The lur
A raucous but spectacular Scandinavian horn

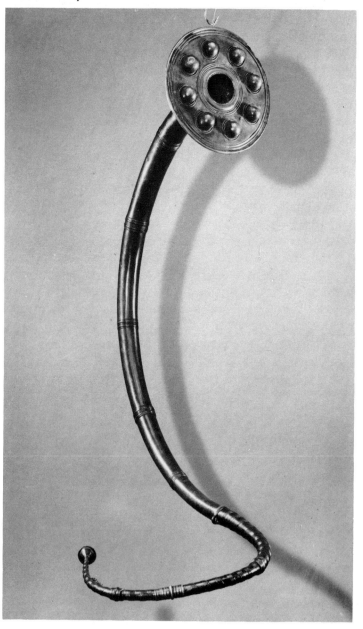

Although the lur did not develop any further in Scandinavia, it seems likely that its influence was felt elsewhere, particularly in the Mediterranean, where not dissimilarly shaped instruments evolved on the Italian peninsula. The Etruscans were also excellent metal workers. An instrument called a *cornu* was found in an Etruscan tomb which bears marked similarities to the lur, and is almost certainly the predecessor of the next development, the Roman *bucina*. The latter is known to have been in use in the sixth century AD.

Generally around nine feet long, a *bucina* was built in a simpler circular shape with a bell projecting in front of the player and above his head. The bell was in many cases grotesquely shaped, into forms such as serpents' heads, and must surely have been feared on the battlefield, striking terror into the hearts of adversaries and their war animals,

A cornu

particularly horses and elephants. The *bucina*'s sound is not as impressive as that of the lur, and so its forbidding appearance was nearly as essential to its function as its penetrating noise.

But a further link between the lur and *bucina* lies in the use by both instruments of a cup-shaped mouthpiece, a shape not known in the Mediterranean before Etruscan commerce spread to the north.

Mouthpiece of a bucina

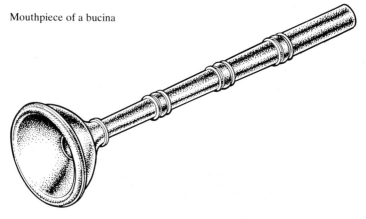

After the absorption of Etruscan culture by the Romans, the Roman horn does not appear to have developed very far, although there was a Greek horn around 500 AD called a *boukina* which suggests that it had its origins, both in shape and name, in Rome's cultural influence throughout the Mediterranean region. There is much confusion over terminology in the records too. Instruments are indiscriminately referred to as *bucina*, *lituus*, or *tuba*. These were sometimes animals' horns, or bronze or brass objects, or at other times of wooden and leather construction. But whatever their names, these horns were still used primarily for signalling or for military and state occasions.

Similarly, horns and horn-like instruments were used in Wales, Scotland and Ireland, but they appear to be poor imitations of the more ancient Celtic horns which had become the more advanced Roman *bucina* in a later age. In the first century AD Celtic Britain knew a bronze

The carnyx

instrument called a *carnyx*, which was also modelled on the *bucina*. It would seem that the only possible survivor is the Anglo Saxon horn still in use to signal the curfew in Ripon, Yorkshire.

The European hunting horn

There was little perceptible development in the horn in Europe. Indeed, if the high standard of the Scandinavian lur is taken into account the progress was retrograde, as the European hunting horn remained a simple replica of an animal's horn for over a thousand years. Metal horns could be made into a variety of shapes which improved their acoustical properties and made them more practical for use in the field. But inventiveness was on the whole weak in regard to their manufacture, precisely because the uses to which they were put were both well-defined and restricted to a pastime which did not demand anything better. Like its ancient counterparts, the European hunting horn was not a musical instrument, but a means of communication. Its short length and extreme conicalness suited the huntsman's needs perfectly; it was easily portable and playable from horseback or even while running.

The code of signals that evolved was rhythmical and as often as not used only one tone, or sometimes two. This extreme simplicity is clear evidence of the lack of any significant development of the horn over a period of many centuries. A thirteenth-century manuscript in the possession of the British Museum describes horn calls syllabically in this way:

'trout, trout, tro-ro-rout'.

There is also a series of line drawings illustrating the hunt in Renaissance France in Hardouin's *Tresor de Venerie* (1349), showing side-blown horns being used at various stages of the hunt together with the appropriate calls. Each picture in the strip includes a set of squares of roughly equal size which describes the rhythm of each call, black squares indicating long blasts and white squares for the rapid repeated blasts. There is one to herald the start of the chase, another to call the hounds and attendants to order, another to broadcast that a kill has been made, and so on. There is even a duet, apparently for one large and one smaller horn, thus ensuring a difference in pitch between the two.

The use of natural local materials to make instruments for communication was not unique to Europe. One example will suffice, as it has great similarity with the char-

Après vehue corneres,
Lorsque le cerf recontreres,
Affin que ceulz qui vous oront
Ases plus s'en esjoïront.
Tous vos chiens hues bien et fort,
Affin que tretous d'un effort

One page of
Hardouin's *Tresor
de Venerie*

acteristics of the horn. The sea-shell, best known of which is the conch shell, was used in the Pacific region but also found its way to India, Sri Lanka, Iran and Europe. It produces a beautiful sound which carries over a long distance. As with many shells, it is a perfect cone and this contributes to its horn-like qualities. Shells played in New Guinea, by a tribe on the Mamba and Gira rivers, use calls not dissimilar from the early European calls:

$-u-u-u$ . . . etc. denotes that a killing has taken place;

$-u u u u u u$ . . . is an alarm call;

$-u-$ . . . is played when the hunter has brought in a pig.

Early horns were not played in the way that is now accepted as brass instrument technique; by present-day standards their execution would be considered rough indeed. Much was apparently overblown with greater emphasis being placed on the rapid passages. Nowadays notes are started with a precise withdrawal of the tongue, but this method was not used in olden times. Instead, the player just forced air into the horn until the sound burst forth, not necessarily on any predetermined note. Once a continuous stream of noise was being produced, tonguing was commenced to articulate the rhythm of the call. This tradition is continued today by bands of *cors-de-chasse* (literally, horns of the chase, or hunt) which meet regularly in France and Belgium.

Early improvements

Exactly when and why horn-makers began to think of ways and means of increasing the range of notes possible on the horn is not known. The usual horn of the medieval period was about a third of a circle. The decision to extend the horn to half, two-thirds and even a full circle was therefore a major innovation and is a step which may be said to mark the modern horn's birth. A wide-bored horn which is completely circular was carved on the fourteenth-century choir stalls in Worcester Cathedral. One of the wood-cuts by the Renaissance engraver Sebastian Brandt (1485–1521), published in the years around 1510, shows a

One of Brandt's etchings to illustrate an edition of Virgil

trumpeter and a horn player; the latter is depicted holding an instrument of three coils which has been looped across the trunk of his body and round his neck. The bell begins its swell at a point behind his left ear and emerges beyond his left shoulder. In all it would have been nearly eighteen feet long, so its fundamental note would have been B♭ or lower. No actual examples have survived from the period, so that one cannot be sure that these are accurate representations of the real thing.

During the following century there was a marked improvement in the hitherto rather sluggish development of the hunting horn. It was a period of experimentation in design directed towards increasing the number and tonal variety of possible horn sounds. It is from this time that the standard of playing rose until at the end of the century it reached its peak and the potential of the horn as an instrument of musical expression was recognized. Its former restricted use as a hunting instrument was being broadened. The French scholar Marin Mersenne (1588–1648) described the four types of contemporary horn in his treatise *Harmonie Universelle* (1627). *Le grand cor* (the big horn) was a large single circle or loop; there was also the *cor à plusieurs tours* (a horn of several turns) consisting of a varying number of spirals wound inwards towards their centre, with a wide bore and of such clumsy shape and weight as to preclude its use on the hunting field; *le cor qui n'a qu'un seul tour* (the horn which has only one turn) was of the shape we see of English hunting horns, shaped like an arc; and, finally, *le huchet* was merely a smaller version of *le grand cor*. Mersenne did not provide any details of the length of these tubes nor of the diameters of their respective bores, but he did say that skilful players could use them to produce as many notes, over as great a range, as the trumpeters of his day. Since much of the trumpet literature of the Renaissance and succeeding era has come down to us, it is possible to form a pretty fair idea of the degree of versatility that was achieved. To be able to play this repertoire, these horns cannot have been shorter than about seven feet and some were certainly a good deal longer.

In 1620 Michael Praetorius (1571–1621), the German scholar and composer, published a *Theatrum Instrumentorum* in which he referred to some trumpets which were 'coiled like post-horns' and showed illustrations of small metal horns intended for musical use rather than for signalling. There are in addition some splendid etchings of multi-coiled hunting-horns made by the Bohemian artist Wenzel Hollar (1607–1677), who was renowned for his accuracy, which give us pictorial evidence of the progress that had taken place in manufacturing standards. There were also two helical horns in the Staatliches Historisches Museum in Dresden that bear out the accuracy of Hollar's etchings. It is estimated that they were made at the turn of the sixteenth and seventeenth centuries.

One of Hollar's etchings showing multi-coiled hunting horns

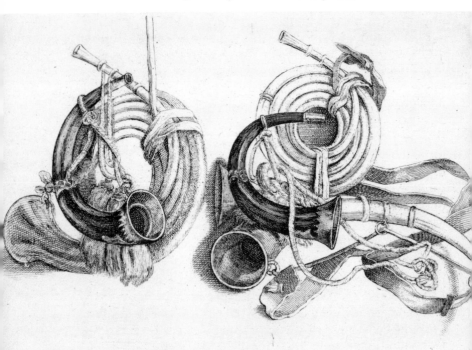

The horn in the theatre

Not long after Mersenne published his description of current horn fashions, composers began to experiment with the horn in indoor entertainments. The earliest use of the horn in the theatre known so far was in the opera *Erminio sul Giordano*, written in 1633 by Michelangelo Rossi (*c*. 1602–56), but the horns are only required to play fanfares by themselves and are not used in the ensemble. Likewise in Francesco Cavalli's opera *Le Nozze di Teti e di Peleo*, produced in Venice six years later, the horns are separate from the orchestra. They were incorporated to provide 'special effects': tone colours and visual spectacle in a hunting scene. Their music was little more than a fanfare, requiring horns of different lengths, and therefore pitch, to produce what must have been highly novel results for an indoor event, although the sounds and sights of the spectacle would not have been particularly new to the audience.

In 1647 Cardinal Mazarin imported into Paris an Italian operatic troupe complete with orchestra, singers and repertoire, in the hope of promoting a taste for Italian opera in France. His plan did not materialize as he had hoped, but some years later Lully seized on the idea to create a French opera. It may be that he learned the use of the horn from Mazarin's or other Italian instrumentalists attracted to the French capital and court and that the design of the instruments he first experienced was of similarly Italian origin. Fifteen years after Cavalli's opera opened in Venice, Lully used horns in incidental music to Molière's play *La Princesse d'Elide*, produced at Versailles as part of a grand fête given for Louis XIV when the palace was inaugurated in 1664. These were not the only newcomers to the stage – bagpipes and guitars were also featured. Five horns in B♭ were called upon for an elaborate fanfare in a number entitled *Air des Valets de Chiens et des Chasseurs avec des Cors de Chasse*. It would seem that the two highest parts are for B♭ soprano horns, approximately

4ft. 6ins. long; the third and fourth horns would probably have been the normal B♭ alto length of 9 feet, and the lowest horn would have to have been in B♭ basso – 18 feet.

In this example the parts are written in concert pitch:

Air des Valets

The scenario also required these *valets de chiens* and *chasseurs* to cavort about the stage in an acrobatic ballet while playing their horns, which must have been an especially difficult feat for the basso player, if indeed the actors on stage played as well; more likely they only mimed, leaving the actual playing to others off stage or in the pit. Lully's directions were for *cors de chasse*, and he probably had in mind instruments like those in constant use for hunting, but simply brought indoors for the occasion. Clearly the horn was not treated as part of the general musical texture, as the rest of the orchestra was silent during the fanfare. The horn had finally reached the world of musical and theatrical entertainment, but it had done so only within the bounds of its original purpose – open-air communications. In fact, if Lully had wanted to achieve the raw, outdoors sounds of the hunt, in contrast to the more highly organized sonorities of the orchestra, nothing could have been more appropriate than the imperfections of horn playing as they existed in the later seventeenth century.

Nevertheless, the manners and culture of Europe in that century and the one following it were set by the court of Louis XIV at Versailles. Horn playing, too, gained from

Les Petites Chasses de Louis XV dans la forêt de Compiègne (detail)

this rarefied atmosphere, becoming more or less a French speciality, of which its name in the English language is the most obvious after-effect. When William Bull, trumpet-maker to King Charles II, moved his premises in London :o a new address in the Haymarket, he announced (in the *Loyal Protestant and True Domestick Intelligence* of 7 March 1681) that he sold trumpets and 'French horns', instruments that are alluded to in the royal accounts of that reign. The 'Merry Monarch' had travelled the continent during Cromwell's Commonwealth, and often visited Versailles where Louis XIV, Charles' uncle presided. A shared interest in outdoor sports and indoor entertainments resulted in the English king bringing back French tastes, including their French horns, after his Restoration.

This terminology was also used in America. In 1772 Josiah Quincy wrote in his journal:

While at dinner six violins, two hautboys, etc. After dinner, six French horns in concert: most surpassing music. Two solos on the French horn, by one who is said to blow the finest horn in the world. He has fifty guineas for the season from the St Cecilia Society.

The horn joins the orchestra

The horn's great leap forward, from hunting equipment to concert instrument, is irrevocably linked with the name of Franz Anton, Count von Spörck (1662–1738), Lord of Lissa, Gradlitz, Konoged and Hermanestec, Imperial Privy Councillor and Chamberlain, Statthalter (or Viceroy) of his native Bohemia. His father, a former shepherdboy who won rank and wealth for his exploits during the Thirty Years War, sent his son abroad to the courts of Europe after he had completed formal studies at the University in Prague. In the cultivated court of Louis XIV he first heard the French hunting horn played in the latest style while hunting at Versailles and other noble estates. He returned home in 1681, aged 19, taking with him several of the new instruments as well as two personal valets, Wenzel Sweda (1630–1710) and Peter Röllig (1650–1723), both apparently organists, who had been instructed in the art of playing them during the young Count's stay in France. These two taught others to play and Bohemia quickly became the centre of horn-playing.

It is unlikely that these contacts were Spörck's first experience of horns and horn-playing. Rather, it was the French style of playing, some of their innovations in instrument design and manufacture, and the more elaborate compositions they performed which Spörck imported to his own country. Having heard, possibly, Lully's opera and similar works, he decided that his own court should in future be graced by such sophisticated forms of entertainment. The desire to be first with the latest Parisian fashions is a characteristic not unknown amongst the *nouveaux riche* of any age! He also brought a Viennese opera company to his residence, enlarging the theatre there and making it the first regular, public opera house in Bohemia. His orchestra earned a reputation for excellence and was directed at one time by Tobias Anton Seeman. As befitted his station in life, he also hunted extensively. To this sport he brought the French custom of using the horn for signalling to an extent not known before and developed the activity into a lavish affair. Augustus the Strong of Saxony (1670–1733) hunted with him and took several horns home with him; the rulers of the Habsburg and Brandenburg houses also followed his lead, so that by 1775 the English traveller Burney could write that 'the most shining parts of a German court are usually its military, its music and its hunt. In this last article the expense is generally enormous.' Thus Spörck's example had helped to extend the art of horn-playing into the sporting life of the German states. Horns of the *cor de chasse* type were being made in Nuremberg, by the firm of Hasse, as early as 1682–9. Mounted hunting with the horn spread to Prussia too.

Spörck's favourite occupations were reading, hunting

and music. According to one commentator he was no connoisseur of music, but his conduct does not bear out the criticism. He would have received some musical education, including simple horn playing for participation in the hunt, and he obviously learned quickly when in France as a young man. He published a collection of hunting songs with horn accompaniment, some translated from the French originals, some composed in the French style. The influence of this and other printed works which appeared under his auspices reached Germany, at least, for huntsmen's choruses with melodies based on horn calls rapidly became popular long before Weber glorified them in his opera *Der Freischütz* in 1821. He worked hard to maintain horn playing in his court but his efforts were not without their difficulties. In a letter to Count Lumberg in 1703 he wrote:

I myself have only two huntsmen who play the horn. Both have families: one of them is already hoary with age and will not be in service much longer; so that at the moment I know of no other to fill his post in order to maintain my musical personnel at full strength.

However his efforts were richly rewarded. The horn was soon found in combination with other instruments such as oboes and bassoons, local playing and manufacturing styles were developed, and the French-trained players taught Bohemians their skills. An important school of horn-playing thus emerged which became so renowned that French aristocrats were soon employing native Bohemians in their orchestras and hunting retinues.

Al fresco amusements with wind bands became indoor orchestral concerts, described by Spörck's biographer as 'princely entertainments', with the horn featured not simply for colourful effects but as a fully integrated musical instrument.

The English still maintained an intense interest in the horn as an al fresco instrument, though, unlike the Central European noblemen with their bands of horn players for the hunt, they required only a couple of horn-playing attendants to maintain the dignity of their households. Sir Robert Walpole employed a black footman, Cato, who came to be regarded as the best horn-player in England. Walpole gave him to the Earl of Chesterfield, and Chesterfield later passed him on to the Prince of Wales and his son, the future George III, in 1738. Cato became the Prince's head gamekeeper, first at Cliffden, then at Richmond Park. Lord Barrymore maintained four horn-playing black servants, and such musicians seem to have been worth high points in the eighteenth-century one-upmanship table.

Sir Joseph Banks, the great naturalist, who had accompanied Captain Cook on his expedition to the Antipodes in the *Endeavour* in 1768–71, refused to go with him in the *Resolution* in 1772 because he considered his accommodation to be inadequate. He had brought with him a large entourage which included two French horn players; their function was not specified but it might be supposed that they were there to add distinction to his position. After the furious row he had with Cook he decided to withdraw altogether from the voyage. He chartered a brig, the *Sir Lawrence* and took the party he had got together for the *Resolution* voyage to the Outer Isles and Iceland. When the party went ashore at Yarmouth, on the Isle of Wight, the horn players went too, and in his journal for the voyage Banks records:

Accordingly we landed with the French Horns to the no small surprise of the people, who little expected to see such a motley crew appear from so small a boat.

Terminology

The terminology used for musical instruments is frequently confusing, although with regard to the horn the French, German, Italian and English names are closely linked to the instrument's function. Thus *cor de chasse* (French),

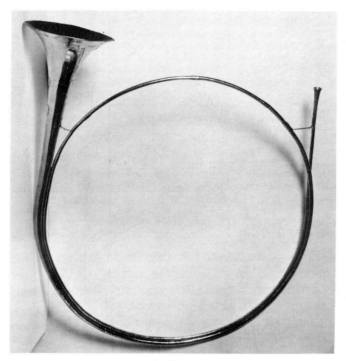

Jagdhorn

Jagdhorn (German), *corno da caccia* (Italian) are all literally hunting horns, although these terms give no information about the shape and size of the instruments.

In Spörck's time the German term was *Parforcehorn* or the horn used in the *Parforcejagd* or hunt. This was later reduced to the simpler, more specific *Jagdhorn*. The later *Waldhorn*, which means foresters' horn, was not really an outdoor instrument at all, but a wider bored horn intended for indoor orchestral use.

To add more confusion, when composers began to include the horn in their music they used a confusing number of different terms in describing it. Bach used several. In Cantata No. 41 he asks for *corno par force*, and at other times for *corno da caccia*, *cor de chasse* and more simply *corno*. He used the term *Waldhorn* in his secular

21

cantata *Was mir behagt*, which was written in 1716, and in the First Brandenburg Concerto, which he composed at Cöthen five years later. But it is in his Second Brandenberg Concerto that the most confusing and conflicting terminology is used. Until recently it was accepted that the solo brass part was written for *tromba*, the Italian word for trumpet. However, an earlier manuscript copied by Bach's friend Christian Friedrich Penzel (1737–1801) wrote 'tromba o vero corno da caccia', which can be translated as 'trumpet, otherwise hunting horn'. But the work was never performed during Bach's lifetime so it will never be known what his intentions were. There is further mystery in that Bach never otherwise wrote for an F trumpet, whereas he used the key frequently for the horn.

Several of his church cantatas have parts for *corno da tirarsi*, or 'slide horn', an instrument about which nothing is known. There are however surviving examples of the *tromba da tirarsi*, or 'slide trumpet', which was used by Purcell. There has been conjecture as to what Bach really meant, but with the total lack of any supporting evidence the mystery remains unsolved and the parts, nowadays, are usually played on the horn.

Advances in technique and design

Composers would not have written for the new instrument any more than the manufacturers would have developed the horn if there were not outstanding players available, and with the increased use of the horn in its new role within the orchestra there was a corresponding development in horn manufacture. The most influential makers were the brothers Michael and Johannes Leichnambschneider, born in 1676 and 1679 at Osterberg, in Swabia, a village near Memmingen which had been an important wind instrument manufacturing town. They went to Vienna in the 1690s and set up in business together. Their horns were not made for hunting but for chamber music and concert use, and were built with a larger bore and a wider

Waldhorn

throated bell, which produced a mellower, less strident tone than that of the French hunting horn. This type of horn became known as the *Waldhorn* and was used as an integral part of the orchestra and not, as had formerly been the case, as an extra, separate feature.

Introduction of crooks. As an instrument of the orchestra the horn had many inherent problems. It could not move outside a single harmonic series, which meant that it was only of use in one key. Even then it only possessed a few notes of the scale. Consequently, when a composition modulated to another key outside the horn's range, the horn was left out altogether.

Horn

It was not until the early eighteenth century that attempts were made to overcome this disadvantage. Provision had already been made to tune the horn by adding extra lengths of tubing (crooks), which was not exactly a new method of tuning as it was already used on the trumpet. To facilitate this the mouthpiece, hitherto an integral part of the instrument, had to be detachable. Previously, this was neither necessary nor desirable, for an outdoor hunting horn built with a separate mouthpiece would obviously be useless if the mouthpiece were to fall out.

Mouthpiece design was also subjected to the same sort of experimentation as other aspects of the horn, for it was found that the inside contour of the narrow end of the instrument had a pronounced affect on its intonation, tone colour and response.

Late eighteenth-century horn with crooks

The earliest reference to crooks is in a bill made out in 1703 by Michael Leichnambschneider to the Abbot of Kremsmünster but it is thought that these were for trumpets. The first crooked horns were probably built in Vienna by the Leichnambschneider brothers around 1710, and horn crooks were certainly in use by 1713, when Johann Mattheson wrote in *Das neueröffnete Orchester* about '. . . horns which can be tuned higher or lower by means of shanks or crooks.'

There are no surviving specimens of these early crooks, but they are thought to have been made in sets of master crooks with additional, shorter couplers which could be added together in various combinations to achieve the right pitch. They were inserted between the mouthpiece and the main body of the horn, adding to the instrument's length and consequently to the pitch of the harmonics.

But crooks had their disadvantages. The most obvious was that each time an extra shank was added, the horn had to be held further away from the player's mouth. Less obvious was the leakage that resulted from the wear and tear of constant usage. This obviously affected the efficiency of the horn, and experiments were made with different methods of joining the pieces of tubing together. The most successful was for the crook to have a sharply tapered end which could be forced tightly into the main body of the horn. This method is that which is used on the present-day Vienna horns.

Crooks that fit into the beginning of the horn are called *terminal* crooks, and they represented an enormous advance in the development of the horn, as the player could at last put his horn into any key.

Hand horn technique. The music of the pre-classical composers and the transition from the late-Baroque style demanded even further developments in technique, if not in the instrument itself.

The horn away from the hunting field retained its characteristic penetrating outdoor sound until the middle of the eighteenth century when the Dresden player Anton Joseph Hampel (1710–71) developed the art of hand horn playing. He had been experimenting with a mute made of a cotton pad and found that when it was pushed into the bell the pitch of the horn went down, and that the same effect could be obtained with the hand. For the first time players could produce all the notes of the scale instead of just those of the harmonic series, and although the sound of the 'closed' notes was muffled, composers were quick to write for the horn played in this way – the most notable being Mozart. In order to put the hand in the bell, the playing position had to be changed. Hitherto the bell was, logically, pointed upwards.

Horns played at the ballet in the upright position, which precluded hand stopping

This was changed to the position accepted today, i.e. downwards and backwards.

Heinrich Domnich, a student of Hampel's who became professor of horn at the Paris Conservatoire in 1795, claimed that the discovery of the hand horn technique was accidental. It may indeed have been an accident, but trumpeters who used the coiled trumpet, as did Gottfried Reiche, Bach's first trumpeter in Leipzig, were accustomed to use a hand-in-the-bell technique to correct intonation. Hampel's reputation as 'inventor of a vastly improved style of horn playing' seems therefore to be exaggerated, though of course the horn, with its much wider bell, was much more susceptible to the technique than was the trumpet, and Hampel undoubtedly was its most famous exponent.

Little is known of Hampel the man, but he was acknowledged as one of the great players and teachers of his day, teaching this new technique to many celebrated virtuosos.

There is a raging controversy among horn players and physicists as to whether the pitch of the fully hand-stopped horn goes up or down. The theory generally accepted up to recent times had been that the sound is raised, since the length of the horn is shortened. If the harmonic series is played on a stopped horn it will sound a half tone higher on the F horn, three quarters of a tone higher on the B♭ horn and a whole tone higher on the F alto horn. The reason for the confusion is that, if the hand is slowly inserted into the bell, the sound goes downwards slowly; on the F horn each harmonic descending to a half tone above the next one down. This means that the lower harmonics can be changed over a range covering several notes, but in the upper register, where they are half a tone or less apart, there is no perceptible change at all. There is still no final argument to support either school of thought, but more and more players favour the 'lowering of the pitch' school, as in practical terms it can be conclusively demonstrated that that *is* what happens.

Much of this confusion is due to the difficulty of controlling notes below the lower middle register. A very strong embouchure is required here to hold the notes steady as it is possible to push the pitch in either direction. There has been, and no doubt will continue to be, heated debate on the subject by players and physicists, but whatever conclusion is reached it is a technique that, through Hampel's experimenting, made the horn one of the most popular solo instruments of the eighteenth and early nineteenth centuries.

Enshrined in horn-players' folklore is the occasion when Sir Malcolm Sargent was conducting the London Symphony Orchestra in a children's concert. He was introducing the children to some of the details of the orchestral instruments and told them how the pitch of the horn rose when the player closed the bell with his right hand. Turning to the principal horn, Alan Hyde, he asked him to demonstrate the phenomenon. Unfortunately, Mr Hyde, who was a mathematician as well as a horn-player, totally disagreed with what Sir Malcolm had said. He stood up and played an open note while slowly closing the bell with his right hand, thus lowering, not raising, the pitch. There were howls of laughter from orchestra and audience, and, after the concert, a monumental row.

Hampel/Punto method. A tutor on horn playing was published in three separate editions between 1792 and 1798, the first bearing the title *Seule et Vraie Méthode pour apprendre facilement les Elémens des Premier et Second Cors*; *Composée par Hampl et perfectionnée par Punto son Elève*. Although this tutor was written for hand horn players by two of the greatest masters of this technique there is no explanation as to how it should be done, the fine details still being, perhaps, trade secrets which were to be kept from the uninitiated. The earliest detailed list of instructions for hand horn playing was written by Orthon Joseph Vandenbroek, a member of the Paris Opera Orchestra. He published a guide to wind instruments around 1800, and a treatise on the horn. It was, however, in an unpublished horn method that Vandenbroek dealt with right hand technique.

He defined exactly how the right hand should be placed inside the bell, making allowances for the variations in bell- and hand-size, and so on. But he maintained that the best method was to rest the back of the right hand against the inside of the bell so that the palm could cover the opening with a single bend of the wrist. He referred to other methods which required the hand in the bell only when stopped notes were needed, but he did not approve of them.

The Inventionshorn and the tuning slide. In 1753 Anton Hampel consulted the famous Dresden instrument maker, Johann Werner, and together they developed an improved horn which became known as the *Inventionshorn*. This was built with a fixed mouthpipe so that the horn remained at the same distance from the player no matter how many crooks were added. The layout of the tubing was altered and two parallel pipes were joined by detachable U-shaped sections. These new crooks were originally held in place by a pin, but frequent crook changes loosened it, and this led to leakages and poor intonation.

Johann Gottfried Haltenhof, who worked in Hanau-am-Main for around fifty years from the 1770s, designed a system in which these sockets and tenons were lengthened into slides, making it possible for the player to tune the

Inventionshorn

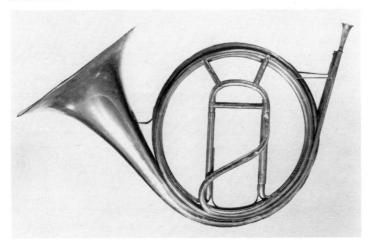

horn more accurately. This was one of the earliest uses of the tuning slide which has remained virtually unaltered to the present day.

Both the *Inventionshorn* itself and the tuning slide were open to criticism for the large section of cylindrical, rather than conical, tubing involved. The hunting-horn that spread through Europe at the beginning of the eighteenth century had always been conical throughout its entire length, as were most of the terminal crooks. The *Inventionshorn* crooks were totally cylindrical, but experience has shown that this cylindrical section has no perceptible detrimental effect on the tone quality of the horn. While many players favoured the new *Inventionshorn*, there were others, particularly in France and England, who generally kept to the horns with terminal crooks, but with the addition of the centrally placed tuning slide. This instrument was for a time known in France as '*le cor d'Anglais*', as it was thought to have been first built in England – thus adding further confusion to musical terminology.

'*Cor d'Anglais*'

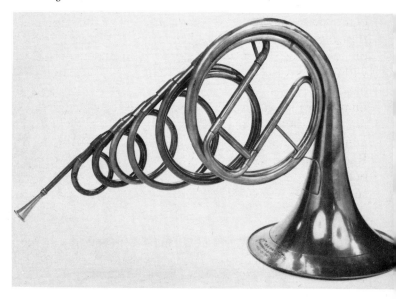

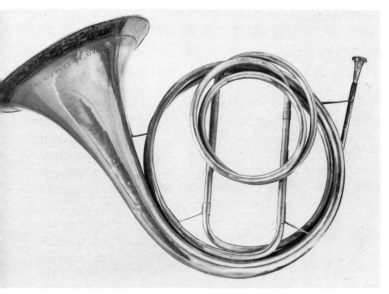

Cor solo

The cor solo. In 1781 the Parisian makers Joseph and Lucien-Joseph Raoux designed a new horn called the *cor solo*, which was based on the *Inventionshorn*. But it was equipped with crooks only from G to D; this covered only the solo keys and it was therefore not suitable as a full orchestral horn. The horn's most effective solo keys occur within this range, as there are a reasonable number of harmonics available without the tubing being too long and unmanageable. These first instruments were beautifully finished with lacquered bells and were intended for Giovanni Punto, Johann Palsa and Carl Türrschmidt. Joseph Raoux elevated the craft of horn building to an art never before achieved and fortunately many of his horns have survived.

The Golden Age

The era of the hand horn players, roughly speaking from 1750 to 1820, has been called the golden age of horn soloists and there is strong evidence to support this. Not only are the names of the players known, but, equally important, there are literally scores and scores of concertos written in this period, those by Mozart and Haydn being the best known and most popular today. But there were countless other composers of lesser importance writing many excellent works that were performed with great success.

This sudden flourishing of the horn as a solo instrument had much to do with its rapid transition from the hunting field, where it was usually and necessarily played in a rough, brash way. Suddenly, it seemed, there were these magicians who could not only tame this wild, outdoor signalling instrument but subdue it to obedience. There was also the unique haunting quality of the hand horn technique, producing strange and wonderful sounds which were so different from what was expected from a primitive brass instrument.

To earn a living in those days a musician had to work for the arts patrons who were rich and noble. Although they were described as serfs, they were not slaves and had a certain freedom. On the other hand, it was accepted that a musician would hold a position in a court, as Haydn did with Count Esterhazy, and with one notable exception (Punto, about whom there will be much to say later on) musicians were beholden to one employer.

Music at this time was the most developed and fashionable of the performing arts in Central Europe and some of the greatest composers of all time were writing music that has lost nothing in popularity.

Mozart had a very close and warm affection for a horn player called Leitgeb (sometimes known as Leutgeb) and wrote the mainstay of the horn solo literature for him. However, the bulk of his horn writing was for the horn within the orchestra, and here he took fewer risks. In fact, much of his orchestral horn writing is quite boring to play and does not exploit the chromatic hand horn technique to any extent. There are, of course, some exceptions to this, but it must be assumed that he made a conscious decision to keep his tutti horn parts simple and straightforward. Even when he uses the horn prominently, the parts remain relatively simple in the exploitation of hand horn technique.

Horns were generally used in pairs, one high player and one low player, the latter usually being the hand horn expert. The custom was to write for the horns in the key of the piece, so that a work in, say, G major would have two horns pitched in G, and when the music modulated away from the tonic the horns would be silent. An exception to this is in Mozart's two G minor symphonies, Nos. 25 and 40. In the first of these he has two pairs of horns, the first pair in the relative major, B♭, and the second pair in G. Between them they are able, using only the open notes, to play all but the F♯ in the opening statement of the minuet:

Haydn also used this device, notably in his Symphony No. 45 ('The Farewell'), where he has, in the first movement, the first horn in A and the second in E. It is easier in Haydn's case to see when he had good players available. When they were, he wrote virtuoso parts, but otherwise he wrote parts as conventional as Mozart's.

In the late eighteenth and early nineteenth centuries it was customary for the second horn player, the lower player, to be the horn soloist, while the first specialized in the high register. 'First' and 'second' among orchestral horn players in no way indicated that the second player was one who could not be trusted with duties as taxing as those allotted to the first horn; there are many examples of the major soloists being low players, among them the great Giovanni Punto, the most famous soloist of his day. Now that hand technique made it possible to play complete chromatic scales from below the fourth harmonic upwards, different skills were often required from players who specialized in the upper register and from those who displayed skill at the other end of the register. (Hand technique is more useful in the lower part of the register, where the harmonics are more widely spaced.) An examination of Beethoven's horn writing will show that, even in his chamber works with two horns, solos are given to the second horn; in chamber works with a single horn the parts are written in the middle, not the top, register. Orchestral horns have always worked in pairs; when Mozart and Haydn wrote for four horns, the third and fourth parts are as important as the first and second and, as we have seen, were sometimes written in a different crook to give more chromatic open horn sounds.

Second horn playing, as it became a speciality, required a wider mouthpiece and a new embouchure, with the upper lip occupying two-thirds of the mouthpiece instead of the one-third favoured by high horn players. The bore of the first horn mouthpiece was usually from 15 mm to 17 mm between the two walls of the rim, and that of the second horn from 18 mm to 20 mm. A first horn frequently used a shallower cup, to produce a brighter tone and a more explosive attack. First horn players also adopted what became known as the 'setting in' embouchure, with a somewhat thinner rim set within the red of the lower lip, giving a brighter tone and greater ease in dealing with the high register.

Experiments with chromatic horns

When the art of hand horn playing developed the horn

moved far ahead of the other brass instruments as a solo instrument. The standard of manufacture of brass instruments also went up, and it is not surprising that further attempts were made to extend the potential not only of the horn but of all the brass instruments. The disadvantage of the hand-stopping technique was that the tone of the stopped notes was muffled and a disparity existed between them and the open, natural notes. What players – and composers – wanted was a chromatic instrument with all the notes sounding the same. Various experiments were made with keys covering holes in the tubing like those on woodwind instruments. One such was that of Köbel, a German horn player resident in St Petersburg, who developed an instrument which he called the *Amorschall* – a hybrid Latin-German word that may be translated as 'love-sound'. First exhibited in 1758, it was in fact nothing more than a horn with woodwind type keys and a kind of lid that fitted over the bell. Tonally it must have left a certain amount to be desired. Keyed brass instruments were, however, used in bands where the tonal difference was less important, since they generally played out of doors.

In 1788 an Irish instrument maker, John Clagget, devised a double horn which, in its essentials, hit upon what became the modern solution to the problem – two horns bound together, tuned a semitone apart and played through a single mouthpiece, with a valve worked by the player's hand to direct the air into whichever pipe would produce the required note. Clagget's 'Cromatic Trumpet and French Horn' won little support as players found themselves in difficulty with the notes in each series which were out of tune with each other.

More directly derived from the conventional horn was the omnitonic horn (*cor omnitonique*), on which all the crooks were built into one moveable slide.

The earliest omnitonic horn was made by Dupont in Paris round about 1815. It had eight separate tube lengths, leading into the body of the horn and on to the bell. At the back of the mouthpiece was a graduated slide by means of

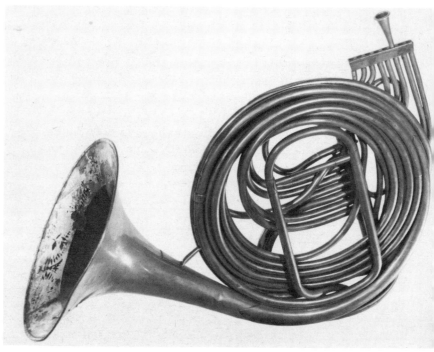

Omnitonic horn by Dupont (*c*. 1818)

which the player set his horn into whatever key was needed; the possible settings were B♭ alto, A, G, F, E, E♭, D or C. The slide into which these separate tubes led had to be pushed into the position which brought the horn into the required key, and a spring catch held it in its new position. Dupont's first instrument was extremely heavy, but he produced a more manageable version in 1818. Labbaye of Brussels developed the same principle further, and in 1824 Charles Sax brought out his improvement, in which each key was obtained by the use of a plunger. Sax's horn did not duplicate the amount of piping needed for any new tuning but simply cut out of the instrument's windway whatever tubing was not necessary for a new setting. Omnitonic horns with various improvements were made by Adolphe Sax and Pierre-Louis Gautrot, who continued to develop the instrument until the 1870s.

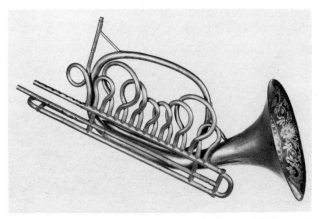

by Dupont (1818 patent)

Omnitonic horns

by Sax (1824)

Key-changing mechanism
by Gautrot (*c.* 1875)

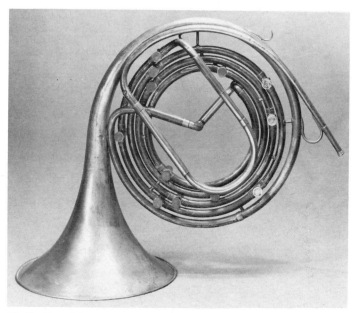

'Radius French horn'

An ingenious omnitonic horn was designed by John Callcott (1801–82), third horn in the orchestras of the King's and His Majesty's Theatres in London. Known as the 'Radius French horn', it had a continuous circular tube within the outer circle, graduated in semitone lengths; an articulated pipe could be plugged in to whichever segment gave the desired key, leading the windway to the centre of the instrument and from there to the bell, by-passing whatever tubing was not needed. The omnitonic and radius horns were very clever ideas for solving the awkward problem of players having to go to concerts equipped with armfuls of crooks. The length of these extraordinary looking instruments could be changed swiftly and efficiently. They could have proved a great boon to the orchestral player, and would no doubt have appealed to composers who felt frustrated with the limitations of the rather primitive crook system. Sadly, we will never know what changes they might have led to, as they were almost immediately superseded by the invention of valves.

One really bizarre way of playing horn music chromatically was that of the Russian horn band. In 1751, the Empress Elizabeth of Russia asked Johann Anton Maresch (a Bohemian, originally Moraczek), one of her court musicians, to reorganize the horn group of which he was leader. He devised a simple conical metal tube on which only the fundamental tone, or on the lower horns also the second harmonic, could be produced satisfactorily. The band usually had 32 players, each with a horn of a different length, able between them to sound all the semitones of three octaves, each player being responsible for one note. Properly trained and drilled, they could play scales and chords, harmonize hunting choruses and even play arias and symphonies. Although the musicianship of the executants was not exploited, it must have required considerable concentration and rhythmic ability on their part during performances. Much of the music was fast and complicated, and a good horn band seems to have owed its reputation to its capacity to play, to order, at high speed, and to fascinate listeners by its articulation and precision rather than by a proper regard for the character of the music.

A 16-man Russian horn band

Two
Valves and the Modern Horn

The single most revolutionary invention in the development of brass instruments was the valve. This simple device enabled the player to change the length and therefore the pitch of his instrument instantaneously by diverting the air column through extra loops of tubing. The significant difference between the valve system and all the other inventions was that now all the notes sounded the same.

Early valves

The first mention of valves as we know them appeared in a letter dated 6 December 1814 from Heinrich Stölzel (1780–1844) asking King Frederick William III of Prussia to use his valves in his regimental bands. He explained that with his new invention he could play all the notes with the same purity and strength without having to use his hand in the bell.

There was considerable correspondence between Stölzel and the court administration in which he repeatedly asked, without success, for a patent.

At the same time, or even possibly as early as 1811, Friedrich Blühmel was also developing a valve system for brass instruments; he probably produced his first working model in 1816. He also tried to patent his valves but, like Stölzel, was unable to do so; and it was not until the two men came together that a joint patent was issued to them on 12 April 1818.

The available evidence indicates that Stölzel bought Blühmel out for 200 thalers on the day on which the patent was applied for (6 April), and a further payment of a like sum one year later. According to the Berlin Bandmaster, Wilhelm Wieprecht, the two inventors had been in contact with each other for many years, but this is not otherwise substantiated; years later they were actually most hostile to each other. There were certainly many arguments about who had first invented valves, but as each had developed a different type of valve it would seem that they only came together for expediency.

Stölzel's valve was not dissimilar from the present day piston valve and was probably more practical than Blühmel's which was box shaped. Unfortunately neither

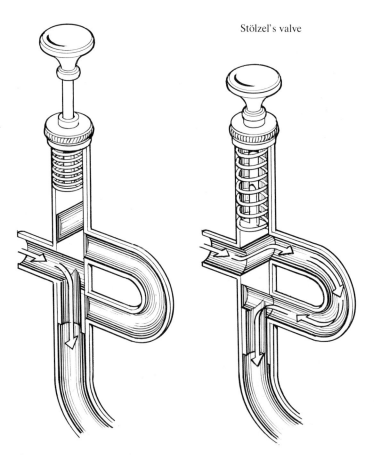

Stölzel's valve

Blühmel's valve

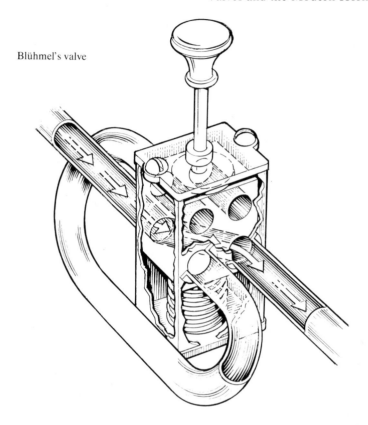

their diagrams nor their instruments have survived but there are many contemporary instruments available with valves that were copies and sometimes improvements of the originals.

It is known definitely that Stölzel was a horn-player from Pless in Upper Silesia and that in 1817 he was a Royal Chamber Musician and a member of the Berlin Court Orchestra. Blühmel was often described as an oboe player. However, this is probably no more than an unfortunate translation of the German term *Hoboist*, which refers to any military bandsman or wind-band player. Their invention had originally two pistons; one added a length of tubing sufficient to lower the horn a semitone and the other

43

was twice as long and lowered the pitch by a whole tone. Used together, the two valves lowered the pitch by a tone and a half. Thus, if the original open horn is included, the instrument could now perform in four different keys.

The addition of the third valve has been attributed to several people, the earliest being Christian Friedrich Sattler (1778–1842). In 1827 a patent was issued in Paris to Labbaye for a trumpet with three valves and by 1830 C. A. Müller of Mainz was certainly using a third valve.

Stölzel and Blühmel continued to experiment with improvements and modifications to their original valves. Many different designs were produced, but most were variants of the piston and rotary systems in use today. There is some evidence to suggest that Blühmel first conceived the rotary valve; he applied for a patent for a rotary-type valve in 1828. But whatever the case it is certain that a rotary valve mechanism was devised in 1832 by Joseph Riedl in Vienna.

Among the most successful were the Berlin valves (*Berlinerpumpen*) which were perfected by Wieprecht in order to combine the light action of Stölzel's valve with the acoustic advantages of Blühmel's. Wieprecht applied for a patent in 1833, and instruments with these valves were in use in German bands until the 1950s.

None of the other experiments were completely successful, with the one notable exception of the Vienna valves (*Wienerpumpen*) which are described in detail on pp. 49–50. This system was actually based on Sattler's invention. In June 1821 the *Allgemeine Musikalische Zeitung* published drawings of the Sattler valve and, apart from a better key mechanism, there is little difference. None of the early valves however were completely airtight, and they noticeably altered the acoustic efficiency of the instruments, making them difficult to play and having a detrimental effect on intonation. Valves also added to the amount of cylindrical, not conical, tubing in the horn and were thus thought to detract from the purity of tone. The windway became even more complicated, with awkward

Berlin valve

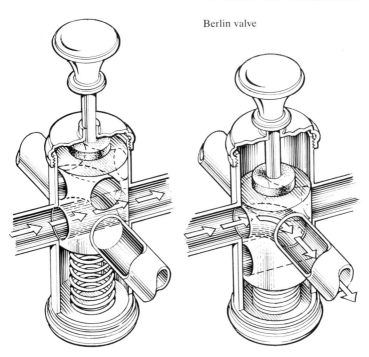

angular turns, so that as each additional valve was added the instrument's response became increasingly stuffy.

François Périnet, the Paris maker, developed a piston valve from Stölzel's valve in 1839, and this was the predecessor of the present-day piston valve. Its advantage was that it gave greater freedom from constraint to the air passages, making the instrument easier to play and improving its tone. An alternative to the piston, the rotary valve, probably similar to that made by Joseph Riedl, also got rid of the difficult angles and constrictions in the windway, and its adoption throughout Germany soon followed. A third system, the Vienna valve, attributed to Leopold Uhlmann of Vienna, who took out a patent in 1830, was widely used on brass instruments of all kinds in Austria, but is now only used in Vienna horns.

These three valve systems, dating from the 1820s and 1830s – piston, rotary and Vienna valves – are the only systems in use today.

Piston valves

A piston valve is based on a piston that moves longitudinally within a cylinder. The cylinder has four ports, one (A) connected to the mouthpipe, one (B) connected to the bell, and the other two to an extra loop of tubing. The piston, in which there are three windways, operates in two positions. At rest it directs the air straight from A to B.

The modern piston valve

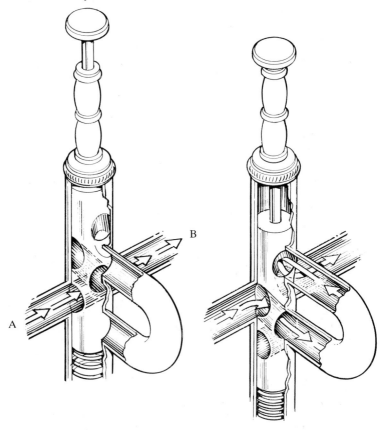

When it is pushed down to its fullest extent the air is diverted through the extra loop, from whence it goes to the bell. When the player lifts his finger from the valve it is returned to its normal, or open, position by a coil spring.

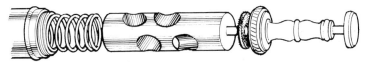

A piston dismantled for maintenance

The mechanism is simple and easy to maintain. The valve is easily dismantled for oiling and maintenance by simply unscrewing a retaining cap; it is relatively light in action and gives a good legato. A difficulty arises with horns fitted with pistons in that any sideways pressure by the fingers will cause the piston to rub against the side wall of the cylinder, so that it will return sluggishly or even jam. The piston system is applied to the double horn by some makers – Selmer in France and occasionally by Alexander in Germany – but it then calls for a more complex design of windways.

Rotary valves

Like the piston valve, the rotary valve has a cylinder with four ports, but instead of a piston it contains a rotor. This moves into two positions 90° apart in order to send the air

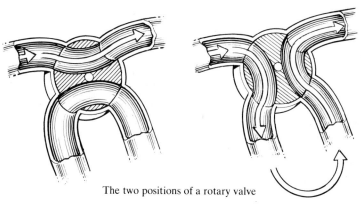

The two positions of a rotary valve

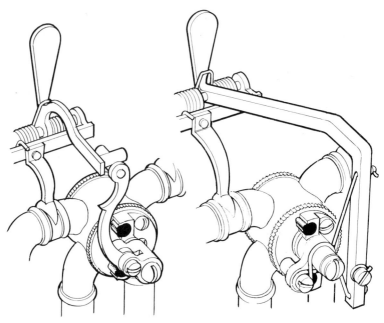

Mechanical action   String-driven action

column to the bell either directly or via the extra loop. The rotary valve is easier to comprehend as it is more diagrammatic. However, it requires a more complicated mechanism for its operation. There is a separate key which pivots from a sprung axle; this is connected to the hub of the rotor by a lever. Because of the separate planes of movement, this lever must have either a universal joint, known as the mechanical action (above left) or another method, seemingly primitive but very efficient and simple, which uses a length of string or cord (above right). The latter system is very quiet and has a shorter key action; its disadvantages used to be that the strings tended to break, but nowadays there are man-made fibres which resist wear and rarely break. Although mechanical action is the more reliable of the two it needs constant lubrication, as the bearings wear very quickly, resulting in excessive noise. More recently a connection has been made using bearings made of nylon or similar substances, and this has attracted many players.

The rotary valve is, generally speaking, more reliable than the piston, though it sounds marginally less smooth in legato passages and it is difficult and time-consuming to dismantle, an operation requiring great care and attention.

The Vienna valve

This type of valve is the most efficient acoustically but the slowest of all to operate. The horn-players of the Vienna State Opera and Philharmonic Orchestra continue to use

Vienna valve

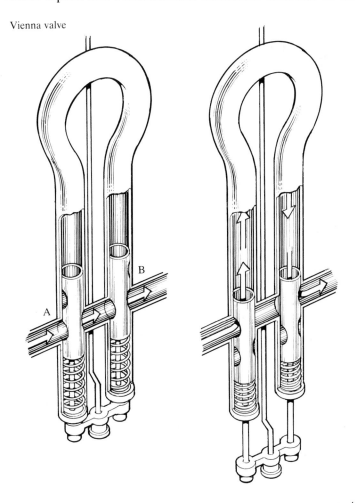

horns equipped with this system in order to preserve the traditional Vienna horn sound, but apart from them it has few advocates. Its main drawback is that with the existing mechanical linkage between finger and valves it is slow, heavy and cumbersome, making rapid technical passages difficult to play.

The Vienna valve is made up of two separate but parallel pistons which are joined and work simultaneously, the first piston (A) sending the windway either directly to the second (B) or diverting it into an additional loop. This double piston is situated away from the finger lever and is joined by a long connecting rod. It could be argued that the antiquated connection between the key and the valve could be modernized, and if that were done the Vienna valve might possibly become more popular.

Problems of the valve system

During the time of the changeover from hand horn to valves the advocates for the former cited its mysterious vocal qualities and maintained that this was lost when valves were used. To a certain extent they were correct, as the early players found difficulty switching to the new technique; also the machinery at their disposal was defective.

Playing separate notes is not so difficult using valves; the problems arise in legato playing. Here the player will find certain progressions extremely difficult because of the sudden change of the length of the horn; sometimes there are terrible bumps between notes and at its worst the sound can stop completely. This is particularly noticeable in an ascending phrase when tubing is added or conversely when playing a descending passage shortening the horn.

The debate concerning the playing of hand horn parts on the valve horn will never be resolved, as it would seem that, unless the composer had the stopped horn effect in mind for a particular effect, he would have found the valve horn more acceptable. The problems and deficiencies of the valve system are more for the players than for the listener.

The overriding problem is that the valve system is not in tune. Each further extension of the tubing should be in proportion to the length being extended. For example, with the standard three-valve system, each loop adds enough tubing to lower the unextended instrument a half tone, a full tone and a tone and a half, and all would be well if the valves were used separately.

Early instruments were mostly fitted with two valves – a half tone and a full tone extension – but that meant that certain notes were missing, particularly in the lower register, so a third valve was added which was equivalent to the first and second added together. Why this length was chosen is not clear; it would perhaps have been better to make the third valve a whole tone extension, but the standard layout continues today, slightly illogically, with the first valve adding a full tone, the second a half tone and the third valve a tone and a half. It would be next to impossible to change things now; all the books of instruction assume the standard fingering, and it is extraordinarily difficult to learn a different system. If a player had a special instrument built with the valve loops laid out in a more logical sequence, the first a half tone, the second a whole tone and the third one and a half tones, all would be well until he tried to play a horn with the conventional layout – and one must always be prepared for an instrument to be damaged or lost.

There is, however, one design, very popular in France, using a different third valve length. It is known as the third valve ascending system. Jules Halary devised this valve layout in 1845 and it continues to be used extensively in France today. Its advantage is that it differs only slightly from the conventional fingering while giving the player the advantage of a higher pitched instrument. For example, the instrument in F with three valves has seven sets of harmonics – F, E, E♭, D, D♭, C and B. With the so-called third valve ascending system, the third valve is set so that the air passage travels through the third slide with the valve at rest. When the valve lever is pressed the valve cuts out this extra loop of tubing. In other words, the valve works in reverse order. The horn is actually built in G, and the valve loops add respectively: one, a whole tone; two, a half tone; and three, a whole tone. The disadvantage is that some low notes cannot be obtained, and the system has found more favour with high players. When it is used on the B♭ horn it is actually a C horn, again favouring the high register.

The Double Horn

In the golden age of the hand horn virtuosos, the best keys for solo playing were found to be D, E♭, E and F. Shorter, higher horns, while more secure because of the more widely spaced harmonics, did not provide enough open notes within the player's range to be entirely satisfactory and produced a somewhat thin tone quality, and while longer, lower horns gave the player many more open harmonics, they were treacherous and unwieldy to play. When valves were accepted by composers and players the F horn became the most popular; though shorter than the E♭ horn it still had the characteristic richness of sound, but was more secure to play and with the valves provided all the notes required in the standard repertoire with the exception of the pedal B♭. As a result F is the key in which most horn parts were, and still are, written.

The F valved horn was noticeably less efficient than the F natural horn and with the increasing demands made on them by composers, the high players (the first and third) began to find the F horn too insecure and unpredictable in the high register. They began using shorter instruments the most popular being the B♭ alto. Many people, however, felt that the tone of this instrument in the middle register was too rough. In addition, with the usual three valves,

A double horn by Kruspe

there were great intonation problems in the lower middle register, and many low notes were missing altogether.

In 1898 Ed. Kruspe, the horn maker from Erfurt in Germany, designed and built the first double horn. As its names implies, it is really two horns in one, each with its own set of valves and slides but sharing a common mouthpiece and bell. The windway starts as usual with a mouthpiece and goes through the mouthpipe in the normal fashion until it reaches a valve operated by the thumb. From here it can be directed in one of two directions. Most double horns are pitched in F and B♭, and when the thumb valve is at rest the windway goes past the three valves of the F horn and returns to the thumb valve and on out to the bell. When the thumb valve is depressed the air column goes on a much shorter journey through the B♭ horn, past its own set of valves, with shorter slides, and back to the thumb valve and on out to the bell. The two sets of valves are operated by a common double length rotor.

The first Kruspe double horn was designed in conjunction with a notable player of the day, George Wendler, who became Kruspe's son-in-law. Two years after Kruspe, the Berlin maker Schmidt made a double horn, but with a piston type thumb valve. (The illogicality of musical instruments is illustrated by the valve system used on some French instruments, where the double horns have three piston valves while the fourth, a thumb valve, is rotary!) Both the Kruspe and Schmidt factories are now defunct, but the remaining instruments that were built by them are much sought after by players today.

A second type of double horn uses what is called the compensating system. It has a basic horn pitched in B♭, with its own set of valves and an extra fourth thumb valve like the normal double horn, but when the instrument is switched to play in F the windway, unlike that of the full double, *continues* past the B♭ valves and goes additionally round the circuit of the second set, which are tuned so as to add the difference between the lengths of tubing required for the B♭ horn and that for the lower pitched F horn. This system is favoured by many players who primarily use the B♭ horn: there is less tubing on the horn and it is therefore much lighter to hold. The system had already been used some thirty years before the Kruspe double, when a 'système équitonique' was patented in France by Gautrot and Marquet in 1864 and in England by Brooks in 1865. The idea here was to compensate for the inherent weakness of the valve system, the increasing sharpness encountered when two or more valves are used together. The system was introduced in London at the International Exhibition held in 1861 and was described by Louis-Adolphe Pontécoulant as follows:

This system can be applied with advantage to the French horn. French horns, as everybody knows, have to be reset for every downward change of crook: by the time the E crook is reached the slides have been pulled out as far as they will go. With the double-acting piston the slides are now pushed home again and a rotary valve is operated, which makes the air pass through a secondary set of valve slides placed at the back of the piston: the combined length of the two sets of slides gives the correct tuning for the E♭ crook. The slides are then pulled out to the requisite extent for every crook down to B natural *basso*.

The virtue of the double horn, whether full or compensating, is that it gives the player the much warmer sounds in the middle register of the F horn with the greater security of the B♭ horn in the upper register; the number of alternative fingerings is increased dramatically, providing the player with a greater field from which to select notes of varying quality and pitch. It was not just a compromise, but a great advance in horn design.

During the 1960s the London horn maker Paxman produced the world's first triple horn. This ingenious instrument was designed by Richard Merewether. In addition to F and B♭ it has an F alto side, with a triple length rotor for each valve. This instrument is an offshoot of the double descant horn, which is usually pitched in B♭ and F alto – an instrument of great value to a high player, but lacking the advantage of possessing a low F horn which many players prefer to use in the middle register. Horns can of course be pitched in any key, but in general the low F and the B♭ alto are the staple keys used, with occasional recourse to F alto and even in extremis a B♭ soprano. The double horn is the most widely used horn today, but many high players use a single B♭, which usually has one or two additional valves added to cope with the problems in the middle and lower register. These problems increase enormously when the short F alto horn is used. This instrument basically lacks a tonal spectrum and has a very small dynamic range, while being the least secure of all the horns with respect to intonation. It has a poor sound if not played well, and is not an instrument to be used by an inexperienced player. Its chief use is in high Baroque music, where a lighter texture is more appropriate, and it should definitely not be put to general use.

Now that better constructed descant horns are available, there is a tendency for more and more players to use shorter and shorter instruments because of the apparent greater security they provide. Unfortunately a very high tonal price is paid. The horn will always be treacherous, and it is really a question of how many risks the player is prepared to take in order to achieve the most beautiful horn sound. The current epidemic of descant horns in the symphony orchestra is regrettable, particularly when they are used by second and fourth players, and is all too often a cover-up for bad technique.

An important, though not entirely obvious, point is that it is not the horn that makes the sound, and that no matter what length the horn may be it is the player who is responsible for resonating the air inside the tubing. A short horn does not make the player's task easier in terms of physical execution; rather for a given note it provides him with harmonics which are more widely spaced and the player does not need to be such a good shot.

New ideas in horn building

The horns built in the 1980s are the same in design and are constructed in the same fashion as those of the 1820s. Generally speaking the percentage of acceptable instruments is now much higher, but with the lack of hand building there are far fewer horns produced that are exceptionally good and the 'Stradivarius' is still very rare. However, experiments are being made in building horns from cast aluminium, combining high precision and lightness. If this research is successful, the whole concept of building metal wind instruments could be revolutionized.

Three
Composers and the Horn

The horn parts that were written during the seventy years after Hampel's development of hand horn technique fall into the general categories of simple and advanced with very little between these extremes. The easier parts stick mainly to the open notes, and only occasionally require the player to correct the intonation or fake notes with his hand. These are usually orchestral works where the horns played a relatively minor role. Much of Mozart's and Beethoven's orchestral writing is pretty easy to negotiate on a hand horn, with the notable exception of the fourth horn part in the Ninth Symphony of Beethoven.

Mozart's horn parts

While Mozart was fairly adventurous in his solo and chamber writing for horn, his symphonic and operatic parts are generally pretty straightforward and need only occasional use of the right hand. The most notable exception is the aria 'Per pietà' from *Così fan tutte*, in which both players have to negotiate virtuoso parts. This is Mozart's only excess in the opera but it does not display the horns as prominently as did Beethoven in the aria 'Abscheulicher' from *Fidelio*. Although most of Mozart's orchestral parts are comparatively simple they still present the player with difficult moments, mostly in the nature of very high entries. The Violin Concerto No. 5 in A is an example. The A alto horn is short, so that only a few notes are available within playing range. The scoring is light, calling for only four winds – two oboes and two horns – plus the usual tutti strings. But there are twenty-nine high E concerts, twenty-eight of them in the first movement.

One of the best known horn passages is in the trio of the third movement of Mozart's G minor Symphony, No. 40. It has some pretty horn writing but is perhaps as bold as the composer ever gets:

The first horn has to fake only one note (an easy one at that) and the second horn none at all.

However, the horn parts in the other movements, though not so soloistic, are very interesting. The two horns are pitched in different keys, the first in B♭ alto, the second in G, with the result that one gets a G minor horn part where the minor third sounds open instead of having to be stopped by the player's hand. In his other G minor symphony, No. 25 (referred to on p. 33), Mozart uses four horns in the same fashion, with a pair of B♭ alto horns and a pair of G horns.

Mozart's first work to include a solo horn was the Sinfonia Concertante KV 279b. He wrote the horn part for Giovanni Punto about whom he wrote to his father *Punto bläst magnifique*. Unfortunately, the version that is left is not in Mozart's hand and it is certain that the horn part cannot be the original, for Punto was a *corno secondo*, or low player. The concertante is written in the middle and upper registers and does not include any of the famous Punto flourishes. Probably what we are left with is a part re-written for a high player.

All the complete concertos and the quintet for horn and strings were for Leitgeb, and it is reasonable to assume that the earlier fragments in E♭ K 370b (K Anh 97, 98, 98b) and K 371 were also written for him. The fragments of K 370b have recently been assembled into a first movement (without a development section) and the realization of 'what Mozart might have written' together with the Concert Rondo K 371 make a pleasant and acceptable coupling, worthy of standing beside the other coupling now known as the first concerto, K 412. In this concerto Mozart wrote a complete solo part for the Rondo but for some reason did not complete the orchestration. He wrote it on 21 March 1781 a few days after returning from Munich and wrote to his father three days later '. . . met my old friend Leitgeb on my first day back'.

There has been much confusion surrounding the first concerto K 412. The first movement, which is thought to have been composed in 1781–2, is complete and is in Mozart's autograph. The second movement is thought to have been written at a different time; like the Rondo K 371 it has a complete horn part but there are several blanks in the tuttis. In addition there are no wind parts, but as the wind parts for the first movement were written, unusually, as a separate piece of manuscript, he may have adopted the same procedure for the second movement. There is no answer to this at present and the version that is played is thought to have been made six years later in 1787, but it is not in Mozart's handwriting and includes oboes but no bassoons!

The famous exhortations to Leitgeb are in the original (incomplete) second movement, and are indeed very funny (and dirty) when read in the context of the music.

In the same year (1802) Mozart wrote his wonderful quintet for horn and strings. This is a much more difficult work than any of the concertos and contains many rapid passages that require a fast tongue and facile right hand technique when played without valves and an equally facile co-ordination of tongue and fingers when played with valves. Mozart called it the 'Leitgeb Quintet' and it is one of the major chamber music works for horn.

The second concerto bears the inscription 'Wolfgang Amade Mozart takes pity on Leitgeb, ass, ox, and fool in Vienna 27 May, 1783'. In the top left hand corner of the title page he has added 'Leitgeb ass'. Only the first and third movements survive in Mozart's handwriting, but the exquisite slow movement could never have been written by a lesser hand. Much capital has been made by the uninformed on the 'fool' aspect of this dedication, and to be fair one should look at the music first and bear in mind that the connotation of it must be in the affectionate way Christopher Robin said 'Silly old bear'.

In the same year Mozart wrote the third concerto, K 447, the only one that survives complete in his manuscript. It is possible that the first movement may have been written a year earlier but there is yet another school of thought that puts its date as late as 1788. It was certainly written for Leitgeb because in the 22nd and 196th bars of the third movement, where there are pauses, he has written 'Leitgeb'. It is not now common practice to play a small cadenza at these points, but one would seem appropriate.

Mozart composed his quintet for piano and winds KV 452 in March 1784. The horn player is not required to play in the upper register at all, indeed the writing in general indicates that he had a *corno secondo* in mind, i.e. not his friend Leitgeb. It is a beautiful work to hear and is most rewarding to play. Mozart was proud of it and even went so far as to tell his father that it was the best work he had written.

It has not really been established quite when the fragment in E (KAnh 98a) KV 494a was written. But it would certainly have been, if Mozart had pursued it, not only the greatest horn concerto but one of the greatest of all his concertos.

The manuscripts of the fourth concerto (KV 495) are unfortunately only fragmentary, but what survives gives a fascinating and unique insight into Mozart's way of composition. For reasons unknown he wrote the score (not the solo part as has been alleged) in different coloured inks. It must remain a matter of conjecture quite why he did this, but an examination of the manuscript indicates that he was having his own private game at the same time as writing his most extensive surviving horn concerto.

The other composition of 1786 was written a month later on 27 July and the only clue to its source is in the dedication: 'By Wolfgang Amade Mozart, Vienna 27 [July?] 1786 while bowling'. One can only presume he was having a good time with his friend Leitgeb, and, between matches, wrote certainly three beautiful duets that are the most demanding of all his works for the player. The manuscript does not specify in which key the duets should be played – all horn parts at that time being notated in C – but as most of Mozart's solo works were written for E♭ horn it is reasonable to suppose that the duets were intended for the E♭ horn. This would take the first horn up to a B♭ concert, but if the lowest solo horn key was used, that is the D horn, it would only make a difference of a semi-tone. So these duets were obviously intended for a player proficient in the extreme upper register. The second part was written for a player with a superb command of the register, who must have been a pre-eminent hand horn specialist.

Twelve duets have been attributed to Mozart but only three are in his handwriting. The scholar Alfred Einstein, has caused considerable confusion over them. His muddled thinking is illustrated by his first assumption that 'it can hardly be questioned that three pieces are conceived for horns – Mozart's way of writing for the Bassett horn is different'. Later, in a subsequent edition of the *Koechel* catalogue, he deleted this sentence and said that the duets should be called 'Twelve duos for wind instruments'.

He was even more confused over the first concerto, when he asserted that the E major fragment was the missing slow movement: apart from being an obvious first movement, it was crooked in E rather than D.

Beethoven's writing for the horn

Many of Beethoven's horn parts are relatively straight-forward, but they often contain perhaps only one difficult entry. Beethoven's Fourth Symphony is such a work. Three of the movements are pitched in B♭ basso, so that even the highest partial used remains well within the upper middle range of horn playing. The slow movement is pitched in E♭, and has only one high note:

Unfortunately, this is the first note after nine bars' rest. It is an exposed solo *piano* entry, which causes even the most secure and experienced player some apprehension. What makes this particular solo such a headache is that those nine bars contain a very quiet modulating passage of great beauty, and the horn's first note is the resolution back into the tonic key of E♭, so that it is an even greater responsibility. The worst psychological aspect is that the three preceding slow notes are usually played with an exquisite *diminuendo* by the first clarinet player. If Beethoven had only continued the clarinet part for one additional note, this solo would present no problems to the first horn.

The Second Symphony of Beethoven has much more difficult and exposed passages for the first horn; they are a few bars only and are part of bridge passages:

It is the high notes again that cause the trouble; although the E concert is preceded by another note each time, it is either a fourth or a fifth below, and this upward slur is not easy. Played on the B♭ horn, using the second valve (putting the horn into A), there are respectively two and three notes in between:

Curiously enough, if a natural horn without valves is used, both passages are much easier to play. All the notes are open and need no correction with the hand, and with the natural horn's better acoustic efficiency the notes 'speak' with greater ease. As in the Fourth Symphony, the rest of the writing in this symphony is straightforward.

Of the remaining symphonies, the Third, Sixth and Eighth have very rewarding parts for the horn players.

However, an unusual feature of the scoring of the 'Eroica' is that three rather than the more conventional two or four horns are required, the normal pair plus an additional high horn. Quite why Beethoven should have excluded the lower horn of the second pair is not known, but as we shall see, he did the same thing in the aria 'Abscheulicher' from his opera *Fidelio*. Another departure from tradition occurs in the first movement where the first horn changes from the E♭ to the F crook for nine bars:

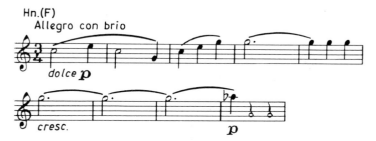

The rest of the horn writing is conventional but in the Trio there is a spectacular section for the horns, the second, lowest, part needing a highly accomplished player:

In the Scherzo of the Sixth Symphony there is a rare example of Beethoven writing high horn solos:

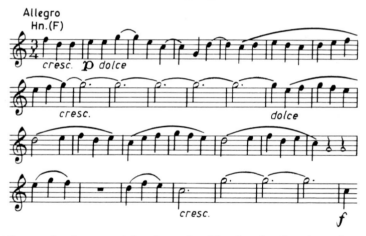

Later, in the transition into the Finale, the first horn has to play a docile signal that is more like the traditional *cor de chasse* calls from a generation or so before:

The Trio section of the third movement of the Eighth Symphony is a *tour de force* for the clarinet and two horns, not forgetting the extremely low writing for the tutti cellos. Here the two horns play together as well as playing identical passages in alternate bars. The Trio is awkward to play and contains several *crescendos* to a *subito piano*, a typical Beethoven characteristic:

The Ninth has one very special problem, whereas for the most part the horn writing is conventional. The few solos that exist are given to the first horn and not to the second, who, when he does play alone, has only a sequence of bass notes underpinning the singers:

Horn

The one exception is the big 4th horn solo in the slow movement:

A legend has grown up round this solo to the effect that Beethoven wrote it for a valved horn, either for Eduard-Constantin Lewy, the noted Dresden player who is known to have played on a valved horn, or for some other player using such an instrument. It has been said that Beethoven would not have written such a passage for a hand horn in E♭; the Ninth Symphony was written between 1817 and 1823 and so it falls squarely into the five years immediately following the invention of valves and could arguably have been written with this in mind. But in fact this is not a remarkable piece of writing for the hand horn, and any player reasonably proficient in hand horn technique would find little difficulty in executing it. Of the eight notes in the B major scale, three are open, two are half stopped and three fully stopped, and it is not too difficult to make all the notes sound the same. Indeed, the effect on a hand horn can be quite haunting. The études in use at the time

71

contain exercises which are far more difficult and complex (see pp. 88–9), and all of the notes written occur in other works of Beethoven. If he had been writing for a new chromatic horn it would seem logical for him to have utilized it in the lower register, where hand stopping is more difficult and treacherous, but examination of the whole section shows this to be conventional hand-horn writing; when the horn does play in the low register, the only faked notes asked for are a semitone below the open notes, and this is very easy to do with the hand. The score also contains the instruction '*sempre corno secondo*', which surely must indicate that Beethoven had in mind the player who was by tradition the most proficient in hand horn technique. Moreover he is following his own custom of writing important solos for the lower (second) horn.

Beethoven really went to town in the aria 'Abscheulicher'. Here, as in the 'Eroica', he writes for three horns, this time all in E. The parts are exciting to play and the result is thrilling for the listener; it is not tutti writing but more in the nature of an obbligato for three horns and bassoon:

Horn

It is curious that he uses the horns so prominently only in one aria, and that as in the 'Eroica' he uses only three of the four available players. Whatever the reason, the aria remains one of the most exciting horn parts in all the repertoire, symphonic and operatic.

Weber

A beautiful work, and one that would be much more popular if it were not so difficult to play, is the Weber *Concertino* in E, Op. 45. Although it is all too often assumed that valves simplify execution, many of the fast passages in this work are in fact easier to play using the hand horn technique for which the work was written, though one variation is very difficult to play whether using valves or hand:

It must be stressed again that this is not nearly as difficult as some of the contemporary études.

Weber must have had a particular player in mind, for, apart from the aforementioned difficulties, the *Concertino* goes unusually high and very low, covering a range of just under four octaves:

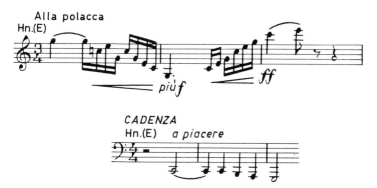

The most noticeable feature of the work is the end of the recitative, where chords are called for. This was a trick often used by players to enhance their cadenzas and was probably thought of as a gimmick, just as it is today. However, in this instance it adds an eerie and beautiful atmosphere to the piece. The version of the *Concertino* available to us today is Weber's second version, and it has been alleged the chords were added later by a player or editor. It seems doubtful that it was a player because of the curious way in which the chords are notated, giving neither indication of how to produce them nor an accurate account of how they should actually sound. The chords are produced by the player simultaneously playing and singing:

and the resultant sounds bear little resemblance to the written notes.

Early valve-horn writing

At first the valved horn received a mixed reception from composers and it is known that the early models were inefficient both acoustically and mechanically. Weber found the sounds produced by the new 'machine horn' intolerable. Wagner's reception of it was not without qualification and Brahms, born fifteen years after the first valve horn was patented, stubbornly refused to write for the new mechanical horn. He must have been fully aware that the players used the valve horn for his works, for at times he spelled out most clearly that he wanted certain notes to sound muffled, or even fully stopped. The following from his 'Academic Festival' Overture indicates that he particularly wanted this combination of open and closed sounds:

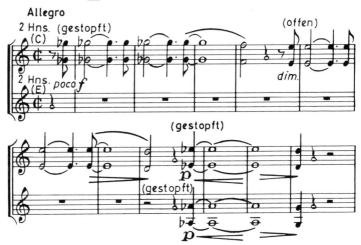

In the third bar of the slow movement of his First Symphony he writes 'gestopft' to try to ensure that the sound is not only softer but veiled:

It is equally interesting to note that Berlioz wrote in his book on orchestration (*Traité de l'instrumentation*, 1800) that

Even Beethoven is very reluctant to use stopped sounds, except in a solo passage. His scores offer very few examples of them; whenever he has recourse to them, it is usually for some striking effect. For example, see the stopped tones of the three horns in E♭ in the Scherzo of the 'Eroica'. [See pp. 67–8.]

This might indicate that in a similar passage in his 'Symphonie Fantastique' Berlioz wanted this harsh, abrasive quality:

Brahms definitely understood hand-horn technique very well as he studied the instrument in his youth. It was his wish that his trio Op. 40 for horn, violin and piano should be performed with a hand horn. It is unlikely that he ever heard his wishes carried out however. Clara Schumann wrote to Brahms after an early performance commenting on the fine horn playing, adding that the player used a valve horn.

It was not long before composers began to be inspired by the valve horn to new levels of creativity. Berlioz immediately took up the valved horn, and indeed valved brass instruments in general, and wrote fully chromatic parts for them, although he still wrote for his horns to be crooked in particular keys, sometimes a different key for each one as in this extract from *Romeo and Juliet*:

Horn

The first major work for the valved horn was written in 1849 by Robert Schumann, his *Adagio and Allegro* for horn and piano, Op. 70. He wrote very well for the new instrument, but was most inconsiderate of the player's

78

stamina, giving him very little rest and, in one section of the Adagio, 28 bars without a single rest. Evidently he did not consult the player very closely, for if he had, he would almost certainly have inserted à few rests without interfering in any way with the work's musical context.

Schumann wrote several other instrumental pieces at that time, and also sketched out another horn piece, the *Konzertstück* for four horns and orchestra, Op. 86. This work was undoubtedly written for valved horns, although it has been alleged that the horn player Pohle played it on his *Inventionshorn* at the premiere in Leipzig. This is actually very doubtful, as the low passages in the slow movement would sound quite ridiculous played on a hand horn and a change to a B♭ *basso* crook would have to be used to make this section feasible. The only other possibility would have been for the player to ask his colleagues to fill in the notes he was unable to produce himself. An examination of this passage shows quite clearly that it has to be played on a valve horn:

Schumann was, however, well acquainted with writing for the natural horn, even if on one occasion he got things wrong. In the 'Spring' Symphony, written in 1841, he wrote the following opening fanfare for natural trumpets and horns:

Horn

This could be played on the horn using the hand, but the trumpet had no way of playing it, so Mendelssohn, who was conducting the first performance, changed the passage to sound a third higher, so that all the notes were open, and that is how it is usually played. However, now that we all use valves the passage should be restored to its original version instead of Mendelssohn's 'solution'.

Schumann's great love for the horn is shown in his description of part of Schubert's Great C major Symphony. He wrote in 1840: 'There is a place in the second movement where the horn calls from the distance as if it is descending from another sphere. Here everyone listens attentively, as if a gust from heaven was in the midst of the orchestra.'

Wagner

The high point of nineteenth-century horn writing is to be found in Wagner's works. He highlighted the new chromaticism of the brass instruments, made possible by the invention of valves, and although the horns were used prominently he wrote only one real solo, the great horn call from *Siegfried*:

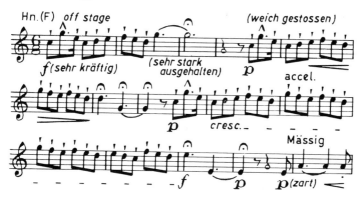

Horn

Horn call from *Siegfried*

However, the opening of *Das Rheingold*, which uses all eight horns, does not use any valved notes at all and can be played on a natural E♭ horn without valves and without using the hand:

83

from *Das Rheingold*

None the less Wagner enormously increased the demands made on the valve horn players, and it is said that he consulted Joseph Rodolphe Lewy very closely on matters pertaining to writing for the valve horn. Although to begin with he had reservations about the new instrument, his concern and technical knowledge are shown by the prefatory note he wrote to the score of *Tristan*:

The composer desires to draw special attention to the treatment of the horns. This instrument has undoubtedly gained so greatly by the introduction of valves as to render it difficult to disregard this extension of its scope, although the horn has thereby lost some of its beauty of tone and power of producing a smooth *legato*. On account of these grave defects, the composer (who attaches importance to the retention of the horn's true characteristics) would have felt himself compelled to renounce the use of the valve horn, if experience had not taught him that capable artists can, by specially careful management, render them almost unnoticeable, so that little difference can be detected either in tone or in smoothness.

Pending the inevitable improvement in the valve horn that is to be desired, the horn players are strongly recommended most carefully to study their respective parts in this score, in order to ascertain the crooks and valves appropriate to all the requirements of its execution. The composer relies implicitly on the use of the E (as well as the F) crook; whether the other changes which frequently occur in the score (for the easier notation of low notes, or obtaining the requisite tone of high notes) are effected by means of the appropriate crooks or not, is left to the decision of the players themselves; the composer accepts the principle that the low notes, at all events, will usually be obtained by transposition.

Single notes marked + indicate stopped sounds; if these have to be produced in a key in which they are naturally open, the pitch of the horn must be altered by the valves, so that the sound may be heard as a stopped note.

Wagner wrote some of the most bewildering horn parts in the Prelude to the third act of *Lohengrin* as this extract will show:

Later in the Prelude he asks the players to change from A♭ to E without even a rest:

During this prelude Wagner asks the horn player to transpose in four different keys, A♭, B, E, and D; and it has been argued that he conceived of a horn in A♭; the three valves tuned to lower the pitch by a half tone to G, two tones to E and three tones to D. During the rest of the opera the horn is required additionally to play in F, E♭ and C so the player would have been very busy, and confused, changing crooks all the time and the possibilities of error and disaster must have been immense.

It is physically impossible to change crooks without a minimum of five seconds' rest, so why did Wagner write in this fashion? *Lohengrin* was written to be performed in

Horn

Dresden, where Lewy was the first horn, and he may have spoken to Wagner about how to notate for the horn; but Wagner can have understood only in a general sense what Lewy was talking about and carried the system of writing for the horn to impractical lengths. Did he want the player to change crooks? Clearly this is physically impossible. Or was he writing in a pedantic form for the new valved instrument, indicating, or at least trying to indicate, which valve the player should use? It is unlikely that the players ever played the passage as Wagner asked, as many instruments at the time possessed only two valves. It is possible that Wagner expected the horn player to change the tube lengths of the valve during performance, but the confusion in the players' minds would lead almost certainly to disaster, bearing in mind that many players at that time were unfamiliar with the new valve system.

Lohengrin was not after all performed in Dresden, so Lewy was not given the opportunity of revising Wagner's new concept of horn notation. But his influence is clear from the following brief extracts from his *Douze Études pour le Cor Chromatique et le Cor Simple*, published in 1850 with piano accompaniment:

In his explanatory notes Lewy writes:

These studies are to be played chromatically on the F horn. The valves should be used only when the natural horn is inadequate for the bright and distinct emission of the sound. When *cor simple* or *avec la main* is indicated the valves should be used as the equivalent of a crook change as follows: E = second valve, E♭ = first valve and D = third valve. Only in this way will the beautiful tone of the natural horn be preserved while, at the same time, retaining the advantages of the valve horn.

In earlier operas, such as *Rienzi* and *The Flying Dutchman*, Wagner had written for two pairs of horns, two with valves and two without, but it was in *Lohengrin* that he seems to have been trying to write for hand horn players who were unfamiliar with the valves in a way that would assist them. Certainly, since the two techniques were running parallel, there must have been many players who needed help with the playing of the new-fangled instrument. This was not the end of Wagner's experiments and thoughts on how to notate for the horn. Later on he also wanted to write for the horns in C as non-transposing instruments, but the conductor Hans Richter, himself a former horn player, was able to dissuade him from it, arguing that it would cause unnecessary confusion. Confusion, one presumes, among horn players, who would once again have to learn another way of reading music – and one can imagine that Wagner did not wish to spend inordinate amounts of time in rehearsing and teaching the horn players their parts.

The Wagner tubas. Not content with writing more and
more difficult music for the horn and trying to meddle with
its notation, Wagner went on to invent a new instrument
for horn players to use, which has become known as the
Wagner tuba. Wagner had felt the necessity of a larger
sound spectrum than currently existed in the orchestra and
was responsible for encouraging the development of a
number of new instruments, such as the contrabass trombone and the bass trumpet. Wagner did not however name
the tuba after himself, but always referred to it in the
plural, *Tuben* being the plural of the German *Tube*
(=English 'tube') and of *Tuba*. But the term 'Wagner
Tuba' is convenient and leaves no doubt as to what
instrument is intended.

He had paid a visit to Adolphe Sax, inventor of the
saxophone, who had already produced a family of sax-
horns, the forebears of the cornet and euphonium, enquir-
ing about new concepts in brass instrument design. He was
not satisfied with what Sax had available and set about
designing a small tuba himself that could be played by horn
players. The result is the so-called Wagner tuba, the tenor
being in Bb and the bass in F. The fifth to eighth horns of
Wagner's orchestra in the *Ring* cycle all have to double,
playing alternately their regular horns and the tubas. The
scoring is almost always as a choir playing important motifs
frequently in conjunction with the orchestral tuba, which
Wagner refers to as contrabass tuba. The player uses his
horn mouthpiece and the valves are built so that the left
hand operates them as in the horn; the bell points to the
player's right, presumably so that the player would feel
more comfortable and to make the sound project directly
out of the orchestra pit towards the audience. The tone is
(or should be) harsh, ominous, strident, primitive and
almost rough, not as deep and mellow as the horn and not
as bright as the trumpets and trombones. The instrument
is not easy to play as the response is quite different from
that of the horn and it should therefore be practised
assiduously rather than left alone until the day before the

performance. Unfortunately many makers opt for a wide bell in order to make the instrument easier to play (bad intonation has always been a major hazard) with the unfortunate result that it now sounds like a lightweight band instrument. The instruments used by the Vienna State Opera orchestra give the only true Wagner tuba sound, which is in sharp contrast to that of the horn.

Wagner in quixotic fashion has added to the confusion of transposing instruments. The most logical way of writing for all the tubas would be in F, but Wagner in his wisdom wrote the parts of the two tenor tubas in B♭ and those of the two bass instruments in F. Not content to leave it at that, in the score the tenor B♭ parts are written in E♭ and the bass F tuba parts are written in B♭ – and all this was intended to simplify things!

The Wagner tubas had their heyday in the period of monster orchestras at the end of the nineteenth century but Wagner used them only in the *Ring*. Other composers have been attracted by the tone of the instrument, notably Bruckner, who scored for them in his last three symphonies; Strauss wrote for them in the 'Alpine' Symphony and two of his operas, *Die Frau ohne Schatten* and *Elektra*.

Strauss, Mahler and Bruckner

Richard Strauss was the son of a famous horn player, the Bavarian Franz Strauss. The early influence of his father's playing remained with him throughout his life, as his wonderful horn parts, not only in the operas but also in the tone poems, make abundantly clear. His two horn concertos, written fifty-nine years apart, also show his expert knowledge of the horn and how to write for it as a solo instrument. Although stylistically very different, they both use the horn in a traditional romantic way. The first concerto was written when Strauss was nineteen years old, just five years before he composed *Don Juan*, and was originally dedicated to his father. Franz Strauss, however, after examining the score, declared it to be too bold, saying that it contained too many high notes, but Richard replied: 'I have heard you practise passages like these at home; now you will have to play them in public.' But he did not; the first performance took place in the same year with Franz Hayer playing the solo part and Richard Strauss playing the orchestral part on the piano. The first performance with orchestra was given on 4 March 1885 in Meiningen by Gustav Leinhos, one of the horn section at the opening of the Bayreuth theatre, with Hans von Bülow conducting, but when the score was published the dedicatee was Oscar Franz, a horn player friend of the composer's from Dresden.

The second concerto was composed during the Second World War, it was performed for the first time by Gottfried von Freiburg, and is one of Strauss's most beautiful works, written in the autumn of his life. Both concertos are in E♭ but Strauss was curiously inconsistent about what key to write the horn parts in. In the first the solo part is for horn in F and the tutti horns are in E♭, while in the second the solo part is in E♭ and the tutti horns in F! Was he being quixotic? We will never know, but all horn-players are grateful to him for composing two wonderful concertos.

In the first concerto Strauss describes the instrument as a *Waldhorn*, which sometimes means a horn without valves. However, the term was often used indiscriminately for the orchestral horn and in this sense it would seem that Strauss was just being pedantic. Unfortunately it has been inferred that this concerto was written for the hand horn, which is clearly nonsense. Apart from the fact that Strauss's father was a noted valve horn player, many passages would sound ludicrous on an F hand horn – this, for example:

Gustav Mahler gave great prominence to the horn and although he did not compose any solo works, he made up for this by writing so many important parts for the horn within the orchestra. He was the first major composer to see the possibilities of the valved horn and there are so many wonderful solos available that it would take a separate book to explore them fully.

The bold opening of his Third Symphony, played by eight unison horns, must have sounded disturbing to audiences of his time as no other composer had ever written such a passage:

Typical of his grasp of the instrument's potential is the following passage from the first movement of his Fifth Symphony. Note particularly how the lower horns take over from the high horns so that the passage does not lose its impetus:

In the third movement he writes for four tutti horns and for one obbligato horn. There is no indication as to what this means and he may have had in mind a different seating position for this solo part. Otherwise he would surely have just written for horns one to five. Curiously, the solo content of this part is much smaller than in much of his other orchestral writing, in particular that in the Seventh and Ninth Symphonies. The relatively less performed Seventh contains two 'Night Music' movements, each with many horn solos. The first opens with a beautiful alpine horn duet for the first and third horns:

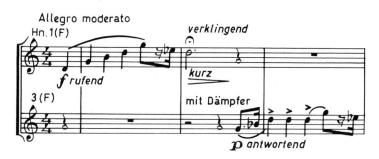

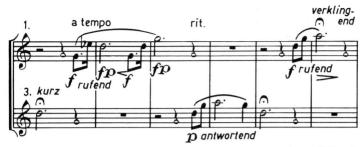

At the end of the movement there is an extensive, difficult and tiring solo which must have shocked the Viennese players when first they saw it:

The big solo in the second 'Night Music' is very taxing if executed as the composer intends, as there is very little opportunity for the player to breathe:

Horn

Perhaps even more tricky for breathing is the solo in the first movement of the Ninth Symphony. It is actually more of a duet with the solo flute accompanied by the lower strings:

This deranged passage just seems to go on and on with no obvious place to breathe.

Anton Bruckner is also well known for his horn parts but he did not write solos so much as motifs. The opening of his Fourth Symphony is a typical example:

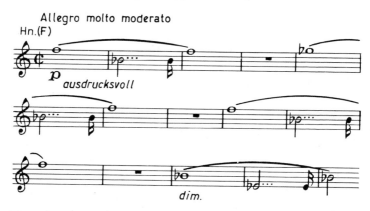

The first horn has the responsibility for the success or otherwise of the entire work, a big undertaking which, if taken seriously, should cause the player concerned many prior pauses for thought. It can be played boldly (and safely) but the mystical mood would be lost, whereas if it is played in such a manner that the first entry appears to come from nowhere, a big risk is taken and the attack may not be precise. However, a musician's task is to make magic *and* to take risks, and every musician should always play as if his life depended on it. In the scherzo the composer is quite old-fashioned. This passage for horns in F utilizes only the fully open notes of a B♭ horn:

Only when writing for Wagner tubas in the Seventh Symphony does he shed the yoke of traditionalism and write fully chromatic parts:

The French Impressionists

It may have been because the art of hand-horn playing continued to be taught at the Paris Conservatoire that French composers were more familiar with the different timbres that could be obtained on the horn. Paul Dukas wrote his enchanting 'Villanelle' as a test piece for the

99

annual *concours* at the Conservatoire, and because it was a competition piece he wrote many demanding passages for both the hand and the valve horn, the entire opening being conceived for the horn without valves:

Later in the work he asks the player to use the echo effect which is obtained by only half closing the bell with the hand:

This effect is not the same as the fully 'stopped' sound; it is less strident and more muffled. As in the 'Villanelle', Dukas went to the trouble in 'L'Apprenti Sorcier' to instruct the player how to transpose his part:

Unfortunately this, and the 'Villanelle' section, are frequently played fully stopped, or even muted, which is a completely different sound, and it is regrettable that so few conductors are aware of the subtle difference of these effects.

Since this work was written as a test piece, it is arguable that when it is played as a concert piece the hand horn section may be played using the valves, and that is how it is played today.

There are innumerable examples in the orchestral music of Debussy and Ravel that indicate the composers' thorough knowledge of horn playing, one of the most notable being in Debussy's *La Mer*:

Horn

There are very few long solos written by either Ravel or Debussy, the notable exception being in the 'Pavane pour une Infante défunte' by Ravel, where he specifies a *cor simple* in G (or G horn without valves). But it is rarely if ever played as the composer asks.

Russian composers

Rimsky-Korsakov and Tchaikovsky are cited as two of the greatest orchestrators, and the former has even written a book on the subject. But both composers ignored the physical problems confronting the horn players, frequently following heavy, loud tuttis with a light, delicate solo. *Scheherezade* is quite typical, the first horn being given only six bars rest before a *piano* entry on a high C concert:

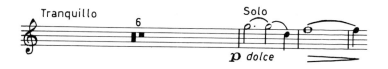

Towards the end of the first movement of Tchaikovsky's Fourth Symphony, which has some extremely demanding horn parts, there is a particularly tricky high entry which, although not a solo, is exposed and is in ensemble with the woodwinds. It must therefore be played very softly:

A more recent example of this unawareness of the player's predicament occurs in the first movement of Shostakovich's Fifth Symphony. There is a long, loud and tiring tutti section which is musically rewarding to play. The first horn, must, however, resist the temptation to take part as he must shortly play one of the most difficult solos in the repertory:

Horn

Brahms

Johannes Brahms is a favourite composer for horn players. His deep understanding of the instrument through his early studies on the horn makes his music particularly rewarding, and his conventional way of using the horn gives the music a special significance. It must be remembered that he was still writing for the natural horn at the same time as Wagner was exploiting the new valve horn, even if, as is supposed, few if any players followed his wishes.

This is not to say that his horn writing was in any way simple. Take for example the long solo in the second movement of his Second Symphony. It is terribly difficult to execute on a horn without valves, but it is also a nightmare to play with valves. It is pitched in a key not very frequently used, B♮, and is very chromatic:

Here the passage is transposed into concert pitch:

The first movement of Brahms's Second Piano Concerto in B♭ opens with a beautiful horn solo. Although this is placed well within the middle register, the second entry is horrendous as it must be dead in tune with the piano, not the easiest of instruments with which to conform, because of its fixed tempered tuning:

Horn

The third horn player has to play a more extended version of this theme later in the movement:

In the second movement the third and fourth horns are given the following little duet to play:

This is not easy for the fourth player because of the long slurred intervals.

The third and fourth horns have one of the trickiest

passages in all of Brahms's writing in the 'Academic Festival' Overture, a curiously clumsy bit of hand horn writing because of the number of fully stopped notes, which sound too contrasted with the open notes played at this dynamic:

The rarely played Serenade in D, Op. 11, has a fine example of Brahms's long, slow melodies. These passages require the highest standard of breath control if they are to sound well:

The most famous of all Brahms's horn solos is that in the finale of his First Symphony. This is not an original melody, but one that he heard when he was in Switzerland in 1868. It is a traditional *Alphorn* melody that so

impressed him that he immediately jotted it down on a
card and sent it to Clara Schumann:

Elgar

The emergence of a high standard of horn playing in
England in the nineteenth century was due to the influence
of the German horn players Paersch and Borsdorf, and it
affected the later composers of that century. Elgar, who
never wrote any solo works for the horn, nor any extended
solos for the instrument in his orchestral works, did,
however, write very difficult horn passages within the
framework of the orchestra and used the instrument in a
fully chromatic manner. The opening of the finale of his
Second Symphony is a good example:

There are some passages in the first movement of this symphony that look and sound very spectacular, while remaining essentially hornistic in their conception:

It is unlikely that Elgar would have written such passages unless there were the players available, and one would presume that he wrote them with the knowledge that the horn players would rise successfully to the challenge.

Modern techniques

Many musicians object to playing avant-garde contemporary music, none perhaps more so than the ultra-conservative horn players. The horn really excels in playing romantic melodies, and a player confronted with a part containing seemingly dislocated and disconnected notes, as in this extract from the Webern *Symphonie*, may feel unusually frustrated.

Horn

Such notes are difficult to pitch, and when a horn player misses there is no chance of camouflaging the mistake by subtly scooping up to the intended note as a singer is able to do. Some works seem to require the player to do almost everything but play the instrument. Effects like flutter-tonguing, glissandos, chords, even sucking instead of blowing, are not infrequently asked for, but with the exception of sucking none of these is new.

Chords. The *Prager Neue Zeitung* reported that at a concert given in 1801 'in several pleasant, partly terrifying cadenzas the artist even blew two or three part chords'. The artist was the great Giovanni Punto, who frequently included chords in his repertoire. One of the greatest exponents of the effect was the Frenchman Eugène-Léon Vivier, who lived in the nineteenth century and was known as the 'King of the Tricksters'. The effect is obtained by playing one note and singing a fifth or a sixth apart from the played note. It has a limited application, as the dynamic level is very soft. It has been used by Dame Ethel Smyth in her Double Concerto for Horn, Violin and Orchestra:

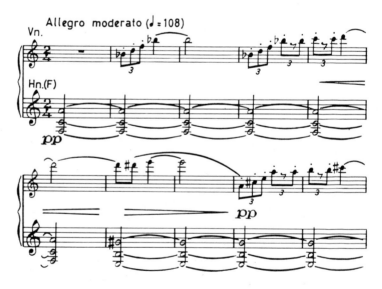

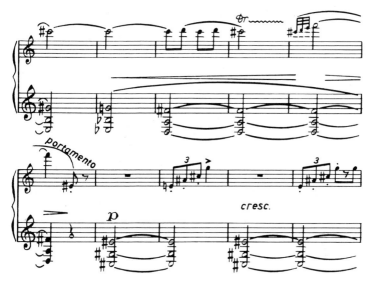

and in more recent times by Iain Hamilton in *Voyages*:

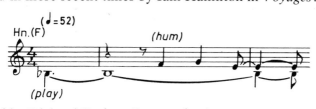

and by Richard Rodney Bennett in *Actaeon*:

Horn

a niente

Harmonics. In the Prologue and Epilogue of his *Serenade for Tenor, Horn and Orchestra* Benjamin Britten writes for the horn to play without valves. It is not clear from the score whether or not the player should correct the intonation of the seventh, eleventh and thirteenth harmonics with the hand, but the two recordings made under the composer's direction should dispel any doubt the reader may have. The high written A near the end is incorrectly notated and does not represent the composer's intention. It should be a written B♭, which, when transposed to concert pitch, sounds as a very sharp E♭:

This use of the out-of-tune harmonics is not a new effect but rather the exploitation of a very ancient way of playing the instrument. (Vaughan Williams also wrote for the natural notes in his 'Pastoral' Symphony.) These out-of-tune harmonics create a mysterious pastoral atmosphere similar to that evoked by the Swiss *Alphorn*.

Thea Musgrave makes use of quarter-tones in her Horn Concerto. They can be produced by using the out-of-tune harmonics, in this case the seventh; although it is not exactly a quarter-tone out of tune, horn players are so used to making slight adjustments that the effect is comparatively simple to master. But because these harmonics are hardly ever used, certainly not in chromatic writing, it is necessary to write out a special fingering chart. This is complicated by the fact that not every player uses an instrument of the same type and pitch. However, on a double B♭ and F horn the seventh and eleventh harmonics are close enough to cover a range of approximately an octave. Most other types of instrument – single B♭ alto or double B♭ alto and F alto – have an extra valve that adds three-quarters of a tone that is normally used to compensate for the pitch discrepancy caused by hand stopping. It is a comparatively simple matter to adjust the tuning slide to produce a very good quarter-tone scale over the entire range.

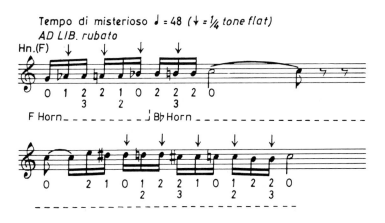

Portamento. The hand can been used for *portamento* effects as well as for changing the quality of the sound. When the hand is slowly moved across the bell from the open to the fully stopped position the pitch is gradually lowered. A good example is in the *Notturno* for Horn and Strings by Mátyás Seiber:

More recently, in his tone poem *Actaeon*, Richard Rodney Bennett has used the same effect for creating quite a different mood. When Actaeon, having been cursed, is being transformed into a deer, the horror of the experience is played on the solo horn:

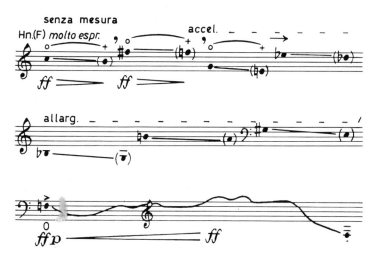

Glissando. The glissando is not exactly a new effect: Punto writes little ones in his Horn Concerto No. 5, as this was an accepted part of a hunting-horn player's technique:

Igor Stravinsky has written glissandos for all the horns in the *Firebird* ballet and he indicates the harmonic series, it is assumed in order to show the players which valve to put down:

115

Horn

Benjamin Britten's treatment of the same effect in his *Serenade*, although it is still fairly conventional, is in a more modernistic frame:

The glissandos that Iain Hamilton has written in his *Voyages* are altogether different and demand a lot of practice and experimenting from a player. On piston valved instruments it is possible to get a glissando by pushing the valves half way down. This is not so easy on a rotary valve instrument, so the player must find other means of getting the effect. Usually it is possible to produce a good glissando by using as long a length of tubing as possible so as to give the player as many harmonics as possible to resonate. But this is not an entirely satisfactory solution for the *Voyages*. And, as an alternative, some fantastic glissandos can be produced by opening a water key:

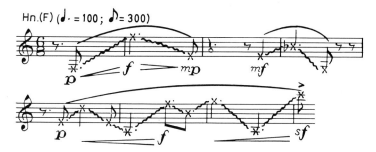

Flutter Tonguing. Perhaps the most celebrated flutter tonguing passage occurs in Richard Strauss's *Don Quixote*, where it is used to denote a flock of sheep:

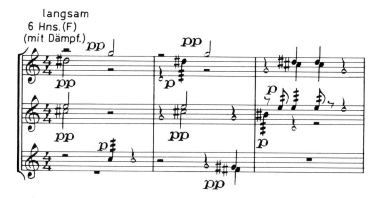

This effect is obtained by rolling the tip of the tongue at the same time as playing.

Other techniques. There are many non-musical effects that can be made on the horn and it is arguable that they can be used as a means of legitimate musical expression. Effects such as tapping the horn with the finger-nails or a pencil or similar object do not have a place in this text, but composers have experimented most successfully with half-valve sounds. These are made by depressing the valve half way to as to cause an obstruction in the air column which results in a curious nasal sound. The notes produced are inconsistent from instrument to instrument, so it is not always possible to play any given note. An extensive list of 'new' effects has been made by Douglas Hill in *Extended Techniques for the Horn – a Handbook for Composers and Performers* (1982), distributed by Columbia Pictures Publications. This clearly lists the type of sound, how it can be produced by the player and how it should be notated by the composer, and is a reference book that should be in the possession of anyone interested in contemporary music.

Four
Some Masters of the Horn

The Dresden Players

Evidence of the extraordinarily high standard of playing in the early eighteenth century lies in the music written at the time. This is well documented in Dresden, where after 1710 the names of the players are known as well as the music written for them.

Two important players were Johann Adalbert Fischer, who came from Pressnitz (now Breznice) in Bohemia and Franz Adam Samm, who came from Arnstein in Franconia. These two virtuosos were given some spectacular horn parts in the opera *Teofane* by Antonio Lotti (1666–1740). This example is from the Naiad's aria:

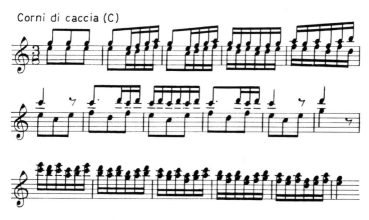

Fischer retired in 1723 and Samm died in the same year. They were succeeded by the brothers Schindler, Johann Adam and Andreas, who like Fischer came from Pressnitz.

Horn

It was during their tenure that Jan Dismas Zelenka wrote his Capriccios; although only No. 5 is dated (18 May 1729) it is presumed that they were all written between 1723 and 1729, when most of his other orchestral music was written. The following examples require virtuoso playing and cannot have been written without exceptional players being available.

Each Capriccio contains many extended passages and only space prevents more being included. It is assumed that, in many parts of Europe, players doubled on both horn and trumpet. This was not however permitted in Dresden.

On 13 September 1731 there was a performance of the opera *Cleofide*, by Johann Adolf Hasse (1699–1783), in which it is known that the Schindlers took part. Though not quite so demanding as the Zelenka works, the *obbligato* part in Alessandro's aria still requires an exceptional player.

Corno da Caccia
(D)

Johann Adam Schindler's place was taken by Johann Georg Knechtel in 1734 and his brother's place by Anton Hampel in 1737. Ten years later, in 1747, Carl Haudek (b. 1721) joined the Dresden orchestra as an additional player. He was a student of Johann Schindelárž, who also later taught Punto. Haudek was forced to retire in 1796 because of some form of paralysis, and his position was taken by his son Joseph.

Anton Hampel. Of the man, Hampel, who developed the technique of hand stopping into a fine art, little is known. It is probably more accurate to say that he perfected the art, as experiments were constantly being made to get more notes from the horn. Hampel was one of the great players and teachers of his day, his most celebrated student being Giovanni Punto. Hampel was a second, or low horn,

121

player in the Royal Orchestra (the *Hofkapelle*) in Dresden from 1737 until he retired in 1764. It is easy to see why he should have wanted to improve the range of his instrument; the high horn player had many more notes available whereas the low horn player had only the widely spaced lower partials of the open notes at his disposal. Hampel also invented a non-transposing mute, the design of which has unfortunately not survived, but it must have been quite different from the present-day mute, as the player was able to use hand stopping technique with the instrument muted. This passage from Beethoven's posthumous Rondino would require such a mute.

One of the consequences of knowing so little about Hampel is that we know little about hand-horn technique in the earlier years. Even the method written by Hampel and later revived by Punto gives no indication of how to hand stop. This, and the singular lack of written evidence from that period, would indicate that the art of horn playing was kept a trade secret. There are many fine methods available today (that by Philip Farkas, *The Art of French Horn Playing*, remains pre-eminent) but until the nineteenth century, a student could only learn his craft from a master player; horn players were almost a secret society.

Other Early Masters

Johann Schindelárž (b. 1715) is important inasmuch as he taught both Karl Haudek and Jan Václav Štich. Not very much is known of his early life but he was first born in Prague in the service of Prince Mannsfeld in 1738 and from 1742 to 1756 was first horn for Karl Stamitz in Mannheim, leaving for Munich where he was acclaimed as a teacher; it was here in 1760 that Punto came to study in his class. It is usually possible to gauge the skill of these early players from the music that was written for them to play.

The horn players at Esterhaza during the 1760s and 1770s for whom Haydn wrote his most difficult horn parts were Karl Franz (1738–1802), and Thaddäus Steinmüller, c. 1720–90. Steinmüller was one of the most important influences on horn playing and teaching. He played for Prince Esterhazy from 1762 to 1772. His three sons, Johann, Joseph and Wilhelm were all horn players (Haydn and his wife were their godparents) and from 1775 father and sons were all in the service of Count Nostitz of Prague.

Karl Franz, the first horn in Prince Esterhazy's orchestra from 1763 to 1777 was born in Laygen-Bielau in Silesia and studied with his horn playing uncle from the age of 9. At 18, he went to Prague to study with Joseph Matiegka. Two years later he played in the court orchestra of Princes Bishop von Eck at Olmutz, he remained there for five years before taking up his position with the illustrious Esterhazy.

By all accounts he was a remarkable player and is said to have had a range of four octaves. He was also an accomplished baryton player and played the Haydn duos with his master Prince Nicolaus. He left Vienna in 1777 for Pressburg (Bratislava), where he played for Prince Cardinal Batthynay and remained there until the orchestra was disbanded in 1784.

Until his appointment as a chamber musician in Munich by Franz Danzi in 1787, he appeared as a soloist in Vienna and Germany, with great success. As with Thaddäus Steinmüller, the overwhelming evidence of music written at that time by Haydn is a sure indication of this player's outstanding ability.

Giovanni Punto. Legendary horn player of the Golden Age of the horn, composer, conductor and violinist, Giovanni Punto (1748–1803) was as versatile a musician as he was famous in his day.

Born Jan Václav Štich in Tetshen (now Žehužice), his family were serfs on the estate of Count Joseph Johann von Thun. As a child he learned singing, violin and later the horn. He showed such talent that Count von Thun sent him to study with the best horn players of the time: first in Prague with Joseph Matiegka, then in Munich with Schindelárž and finally in Dresden with Hampel and Haudek.

After completing his studies, he returned to the service of Count von Thun, but serfdom did not suit his temperament. The few surviving documents indicate that he had a dominant and volatile personality. Ernst Gerber said 'his lord would not permit him to carry a sword and even threatened him with a uniform as often as he let his temper get the best of him'.

So he defected, when he was twenty, with four other musicians. The furious Count sent his soldiers in pursuit with orders to knock out the horn player's front teeth so that he could never play again. Fortunately, he eluded the soldiers and escaped over the border into the Holy Roman Empire, where he italianized his name and became Giovanni Punto.

The first position Punto held after leaving Bohemia was in the orchestra of the Prince of Hechingen. From there he went to Mainz but left when he was not made concertmaster. He then began to travel through Europe as a soloist, playing in Hungary, Italy, Spain, France and London (on three occasions). Charles Burney heard him play in 1772 in Coblenz and wrote: 'The Elector has a good band, in which M. Ponta [*sic*], the celebrated French horn player from Bohemia, whose taste and astonishing execution were lately so much applauded in London, is a performer.'

Punto returned to London in 1777 and was invited to teach the horn players in the private orchestra of King

George III. The King must have had a special interest in the horn as, some thirty years earlier, as the Prince of Wales, he had employed a black footman, Cato, who was regarded as the best horn player in England.

On his next visit to London in 1788 he performed at Gertrud Elisabeth Mara's vocal concerts at the Pantheon, described by Michael Kelly in his *Reminiscences of the King's Theatre and Theatre Royal Drury Lane*:

I went one oratorio night into the green room to speak to Mrs Crouch but the only persons in the room were Madame Mara and Monsieur Ponte [*sic*], the first horn player to the King of Prussia, and a very fine performer; he was an intimate friend of Madame Mara, and engaged to play a concerto . . . that night. He said to Madame Mara in German 'My dear friend, my lips are so parched with fear that I am sure that I shall not make a sound in the instrument; I would give the world for a little water or beer to moisten my lips.' Madame Mara replied in German 'There is nobody here to send; and yet if I knew where to get something for you to drink, I would go myself.'

During their dialogue, I was standing at the fireside, and addressing Madame Mara in German, I said, 'Madame, I should be sorry for you to have that trouble, and I sit lazy by. I will, with great pleasure, go and get Monsieur Ponte some Porter.'

I instantly dispatched a messenger for a foaming pot; and as soon as it arrived. I presented it to the thirsty musician, in the nick of time, for he was called on to play his concerto just at this moment.

Punto was moving around Europe throughout this period, playing as a soloist and with different court orchestras. In 1778 when he was in Paris he met Mozart, who wrote to his father saying '*Punto bläst magnifique!*' And it was for Punto and three colleagues that Mozart wrote the Sinfonia Concertante KV 279b.

Although Punto was in great demand as a horn player, he wished for a secure position or patronage and a chance to conduct and play the violin. In 1781 he went in to the service of Prince Archbishop of Wurzburg, but left to go as concert-master, with a pension, for the Count d'Artois (later Charles X) in Paris. He spent many years in Paris and the French historian François J. Fétis wrote that his father, having heard Punto play, remarked how 'One cannot imagine a more beautiful sound, a greater assurance of attack, or a more moving manner of phrasing.'

Obtaining leave of absence from the Count d'Artois in 1788, Punto made a concert tour of Germany in his own coach, which gives us an idea of his success and prosperity. Back in Paris in the Reign of Terror he was pleased to be given the post of violinist and conductor at the Théâtre des Variétés Amusantes, but in 1799 after having apparently tried unsuccessfully to get on the staff of the newly founded Conservatoire, went to Vienna.

In Vienna he met Beethoven, who wrote the Sonata Op. 17 for him. It had its first performance in April 1800 in the Burgtheater with the composer playing the piano. The following month they played it again in Pest (now Budapest), where the music critic wrote 'Who is this Beethover [*sic*]? His name is not known in musical circles. Of course Punto is very well known.'

After thirty-three years' absence, Punto returned triumphantly to his homeland in 1801, playing in the Prague National Theatre where, wrote Diabacz, 'His prodigious skill was admired by the entire audience.' According to the *Pragerneue Zeitung:*

Punto received enthusiastic applause for his concertos because of his unparalleled mastery, and respected musicians said that they had never before heard horn playing like it. This performance on a usually clumsy instrument sang out in all registers. In his cadenzas he produced many novel effects, playing two- and even three-part chords. It demonstrated again that our fatherland can produce great artistic and musical geniuses.

It was at this time that he became friendly with the composer-pianist Dusseh, with whom he toured his native Bohemia, including his birthplace, giving many recitals. After a short trip to Paris in 1802 he developed pleurisy, from which he died in Prague on 16 February 1803. On 26

February a magnificent funeral mass was held in the Church of St Nicholas, before, it was said, thousands of people, so great was Punto's fame. His tomb had the following verse inscribed on it:

Omne tulit punctum Punto, cui Musa Bohema
Ut plausit vivo, sic morienti gemit.

Punto received all the applause. Just as the Muse of Bohemia applauded him in life, so she did mourn him in death.

Like many players of his time, Punto composed pieces to display his own vituosity. With a couple of exceptions, all of Punto's compositions were for the horn.

German players of the late eighteenth century

The number of outstanding players at this time is quite staggering and the Türrschmidt family is worthy of special attention. Johannes Türrschmidt (1725–1800) was the father of the celebrated Carl Türrschmidt. The earliest reference to his career is when he was appointed first horn in the orchestra of Prince Kraft Ernst of Oettingen-Wallterstein in 1752, where he remained for 28 years. It was during this period that Haydn wrote his symphonies Nos. 46, 47 and 48 for the Prince and the very difficult horn parts are a great tribute to Johannes Türrschmidt's exceptional ability. Anton Rosetti wrote high horn concertos for him and from this evidence alone we can be sure that he was a player of the highest order. His two brothers, Joseph and Anton, also played the horn and his grandson (son of Carl) is known to have been an excellent player.

Carl Türrschmidt. Carl Türrschmidt (1753–97) was an outstanding soloist and a great friend and colleague of Punto. He was a *corno secondo*, or low horn player. Anton Rosetti wrote his fine low horn concertos for him. His technical ability was astonishing, in particular his right-hand technique, and he was also noted for his beauty of tone.

He was the low half of a celebrated duo with the horn player Johann Palsa (1752–92) with whom he made many tours, going as far afield as Paris and London. They both held posts in Paris with the orchestra of Prince de Rohan-Guémenée until 1783, when the Prince went bankrupt and they moved to Kassel, remaining there until 1786 when they moved to Berlin.

Carl Türrschmidt played on a silver Raoux, one of three made in 1781; the others were for Palsa and Punto. He was active as a designer of horns, also of mutes, perfecting the non-transposing mute used by Hampel that could be made to alter the harmonics in a manner similar to hand stopping. His son, the third generation of this horn-playing dynasty, continued the family tradition and was also known to be an excellent player.

Spandau. Spandau was first horn in the Hague Electoral orchestra, and is said to have been the first player to have played the hand horn in England, in 1773. Burney was most impressed by him and wrote that he

continued in his performance so to correct the natural imperfections of the horn, as to make it a chamber instrument. He played in all keys, with an equality of tone, and as much accuracy of intonation in the chromatic notes, as could be done on a violin – by which means in his delicacy, taste, and expression, he rendered an instrument which, from its force and coarseness, could formerly be only supported in the open air in theatres or spacious buildings, equally soft and pleasing with the human voice.

Christian Shubart in 1785 called him 'the foremost player of our time' but regretted that the notes sometimes split in the high register – an observation that still appeals to many critics.

Ignaz Leitgeb. Most of Mozart's solo music for horn was written for his lifelong friend Ignaz Leitgeb. This name has been spelt in a variety of ways including Liekhgeb and

Seikgeb. He was also known as Leutgeb, but as Mozart wrote 'Leitgeb' in his concertos this is the spelling used here. He was probably born in Salzburg around 1745, and played there at the same time as Mozart, before moving to Vienna.

Poor Leitgeb has been much maligned over the years by writers who have assumed that he was a stupid man. This is because of the ribald remarks written in Mozart's sketch for what has become known as the second movement of the D major concerto. The same has not been said about his cousin to whom Wolfgang wrote obscene, scatalogical letters.

Leitgeb was undoubtedly a fine player as, apart from the music that Mozart wrote for him, there is evidence of his musical and technical prowess provided by the critics of the time. After he played in Paris in 1770 the *Mercure de France* of April/May remarked on 'the applause being deserved because of the superior talent he showed in the performance of his own concerto'. And again later 'The tone that he produces is a continuous source of wonder to his listeners. His most outstanding quality is to be able to 'sing' in the adagios as perfectly as the most mellow, the most interesting and the most accurately pitched human voice.' He appeared the same year in Frankfurt where the *Postzeitung* wrote how

Our city is honoured that the most famous artists and virtuosos choose it as an arena in which to display their accomplishments and talents. Recently, we had the good fortune to admire Mr Holtzbogen in a concert – as well as Mr Leutgeb on the horn, from Salzburg, already known in these parts. Both artists are of such exceptional calibre that they received applause from the entire audience.

After Leitgeb arrived in Vienna he borrowed some money from Leopold Mozart to open a cheese shop which was so tiny that Leopold Mozart wrote to his son Wolfgang that 'Mr Leitgeb, who has bought a cheese shop the size of a snail's shell, wrote to us after you left promising to pay me eventually and asked you for a concerto.' It appears that Leitgeb was somewhat dilatory over repaying the loan, for four-and-a-half years later, on 8 May 1782, Wolfgang wrote to his father

Please be patient with poor Leitgeb. If you knew his circumstances and saw how he has to muddle along you would certainly have sympathy for him. I shall speak to him and I feel sure he will pay you, even if it is by instalments.

There are many references to each staying with the other, and Mrs Leitgeb even did Mozart's washing. After Mozart's death it was Leitgeb who helped Constance Mozart to sort out all his manuscripts.

Another injustice to the memory of Leitgeb is the jibe that he was 'cheesemonger'. Actually, when he died he was a highly successful merchant, as was the famous violinist Viotti, who at the height of his career went into the wine business.

Nineteenth-century players

The Golden Age of horn-playing continued into the nineteenth century and Bohemia was the birthplace of the brothers Petrides, John and Peter, who came from Prague and settled in London in 1802; they stayed there until 1824 and greatly influenced horn-playing in England. They had toured throughout Europe, in Germany, Austria, France, Spain and Portugal, for fifteen years from 1784, during which time they were shipwrecked more than once, which (one assumes) put their baggage and therefore their instruments at constant risk! They arrived in England with letters of introduction to the Duke of Sussex and made their debut in Willis's Rooms in a benefit concert for Salomon. One observer (*Musical Recollections*, edited by the Rev'd. J. E. Cox and published in 1872) noted that these 'much admired performers on the horn' were 'the quaintest beings that ever entered an orchestra, and who, in the interval of a bar or two's rest, amused themselves by kicking each other's shins, since they could not quarrel more uproariously'. Ella's *Musical Sketches Abroad and at Home* of 1878 gives an interesting picture of them:

In 1822 the French horns in the band of Her Majesty's Theatre were played by the above two venerable Bohemians. In dress and appearance they resembled each other – both wearing pants fitting tight down to the ankles, a brown wig, an oddly shaped hat, and large green spectacles. When accused, at rehearsals, of playing a wrong note, each would answer *'was mein Brüder'*; until the copyist discovered that the parts were wrong, and neither of the brethren was at fault, they would snarl and utter unkind expressions towards each other, with a menacing look. At other times they were the most united of brothers.

Giovanni Puzzi. Another player active in London during the same period was the Italian Giovanni Puzzi (b. Parma 1792; d. London 1876), who followed in the steps of that other Giovanni, Punto, from the point of view of virtuosity and the colourful life he led. His playing set standards of excellence all over Europe. One critic wrote: 'It would be invidious to distinguish one performer more than another, yet I cannot help remarking, that the first horn-player has an exquisite tone, and as much command of his instrument as Puzzi; can praise go higher?' He played at the Opéra Comique in 1830 and was known as 'a fashionable player', so great was his celebrity in continental society. Weber called him 'the renowned Puzzi' and Fétis said of him that he was so remarkably talented and had made such a fortune by his playing that he was able to play as a soloist, not as an orchestral musician!

But his residence and performances in England were the factors which provide so much of his biographical history. Puzzi was for a long time associated with the King's Theatre in London. In 1826 its manager, Ebers, asked Puzzi to go to Europe to engage singers for an Italian opera season in London. One of these was Giacinta Toso whom he married a few months after bringing her back to England. Puzzi played less and less as he became involved in the promotion of the arts as an impresario. The main horn-player at the King's Theatre was Edward Platt (1793–1861); Puzzi was the soloist and virtuoso. Platt was said to have deputized for Puzzi on occasion, although not as spectacularly: 'Mr Platt has yet to learn how to perform on his obstreperous instrument in a concert-room: there is no necessity to puff out one's cheeks, or blow until the hearer feels a sympathetic sense of pity for the performer,' wrote the critic for *The Musical World*, 8 March 1838. Two weeks later the same periodical reported that 'Mr Platt and his co-adjutors should be taught by the conductor that there is a difference between *sf* and *ff*. Again and again the unwearied exertions of these rude sons of Boreas smothered every component part of the harmony save their own open notes' But years later Costa was reported in the *Illustrated London News* (20 April 1850) as having said of the same performer that 'in singing on the horn, it was the finest and most genuine tone' he had ever heard.

Heinrich Domnich. London was not the only city to import its horn players from abroad. One of the most important players and teachers in Paris was the Bavarian Heinrich Domnich (1767–1844). He was one of a great family of horn players; his father and two brothers all played. He was playing concertos when he was 12 years old and at 18 rebelled at the servitude required and left for Paris, where he met and studied with Punto. He joined the Opera orchestra as a second horn in 1787 and was appointed to the Conservatoire as horn professor in 1795, remaining there until 1817. He wrote an important method, three horn concertos, two concertantes for two horns, and many songs. Of his two brothers the older, Jacob, emigrated to the United States where he settled, played and taught in Philadelphia. The younger brother Arnold was first horn at the Court of Sachsen Meinigen.

French players. Domnich's contemporary and even more celebrated and famous colleague was Frédéric-Nicolas

ACADEMIE IMPERIALE
DE MUSIQUE.

On commencera à sept heures précises. — Aujourd'hui mardi 15 décembre 1807,

LA PREMIERE REPRESENTATION DE

LA VESTALE,

Opéra en trois actes

M. *FREDERIC DUVERNOY* exécutera les Solos de Cor.

Chant : Mrs. *Lainez, Lays, Dérivis, Duparc, Martin ;* Mmes. *Maillard, Branchu.*

Danse : Mrs. *Vestris, Beaulieu, St.-Amand, Branchu, Baptiste Petit ;* Mmes. *Clotilde, Gardel, Chevigny, Millière, Bigottini, Vestris, Mareiller* cadette, *Riviere, Mareiller* ainée.

S'adresser pour la location des Loges, à M. *Damence*, à la Salle de l'Académie impériale de Musique.

Les billets une fois pris, on n'en rendra plus la valeur.

Duvernoy (1765–1838), soloist at the Concert Spirituel and later at the Paris Opéra. Duvernoy, said to have been self-taught, was a *cor mixte* (or both high and low player) and a great favourite with the public. The advertisement for the premiere of Gasparo Spontini's opera *La Vestale* announced in large type that '*M. FREDERIC DUVERNOY éxécutera les Solos du Cor.*' while the singer's names – surnames only – were in smaller type and Spontini's name did not appear at all! Duvernoy became senior professor of the horn at the Paris Conservatoire in 1795, the same year that Domnich was appointed. He wrote perhaps the greatest method of his time, as well as five concertos, several charming concert pieces for horn and piano, and a number of études and works for horn ensembles.

Another notable French horn soloist and composer was Victor Pélissier, who settled in Philadelphia in 1792 and later moved to New York: and another, a pioneer of hand horn technique, was Jean-Joseph Rodolphe, born in Strasbourg in 1730. Although already celebrated as a horn virtuoso, it seems that he joined the Paris Opera orchestra in 1765 as a violinist, playing the horn only in solos. He was professor of composition at the École Royale de Chant from 1784 to 1788 and professor of *solfège* when the Conservatoire was formed in 1798. He died in 1812 at the age of 82.

Pioneers of the valve horn

In the 1820s the era of the hand-horn virtuosos began to draw to a close. This was no sudden transformation; by 1850 or thereabouts all the handhorn soloists of international repute still living were well past their prime, while the valve horn had still not as yet quite emerged from the experimental stage. Horns with two valves were still in use up to and beyond the middle of the century.

Pierre Joseph Emile Meifred. Among the most important of the valve-horn pioneers in France was Pierre Joseph Emile Meifred (1791–1867). He was the first French horn player to devote himself exclusively to the valve horn, which France was slow to take up. He improved the valve mechanism in collaboration with Jacques-Charles Labbaye, by adding slides to the valve loops, and in 1833 became professor at the Paris Conservatoire when the first valve-horn class was established. His *Méthode pour le Cor Chromatique* was written for the horn with two valves. He held that a two-valve horn, with the use of crooks and of hand stopping techniques, could produce a chromatic scale with good intonation and good tone throughout, and he remained faithful to the two-valve instrument until the appearance of the ascending third valve system developed by Jules Halary, one of his pupils, in about 1847.

The Lewy brothers. Reference has already been made to the German Lewy brothers, Eduard Constantin

(1796–1846) and Joseph Rodolphe (1804–81), both of whom were able to help composers understand the valve horn. Eduard Constantin studied horn with Heinrich Domnich as a boy, and also the violin and cello at the Paris Conservatoire. He became principal horn in the Vienna Imperial Orchestra in 1822, but continued to make tours as a solo artist; he was appointed professor of the horn at the Vienna Conservatory in 1834 and died, only fifty years old, in 1846.

Nicolaus Simrock (1755–1818) is perhaps best remembered as the founder of the great publishing house which bore his name. But he started his musical life in 1773 as first horn with the Court orchestra in Cologne. Five years later he moved to Bonn and it was during his twelve years there that he became close friends with a viola player in the same orchestra called Ludwig van Beethoven.

Franz Strauss (1822–1905), whose family had been in the police force since 1700, was born at Parkstein in Bavaria and brought up in a musical environment by his mother, the daughter of the watchman of the Tower at Parkstein, who numbered among his duties that of playing the trumpet. Young Franz learned to play the clarinet, guitar, trumpet, trombone and horn from his uncle, having started his career on the violin at the age of five. When he was nine he actually gave instruction in these instruments as well as playing in his uncle's band. At fifteen he began a ten-year period of service to the Duke Max of Bavaria in Munich as an instrumentalist in his court orchestra, but it was the horn that interested him most and in 1847 he joined the Bavarian Court orchestra and played in concerts and opera for the next forty years. His first wife died of cholera and Strauss remained unmarried for ten years, but in 1863 he married Josephine, daughter of a brewer, Georg Pschorr, and their famous son Richard was born the following year.

Strauss senior – Bülow called him 'the Joachim of the

horn' – wrote a lot of music for the horn and performed his own horn concerto Op. 8 in 1865. His musical tastes were conservative, and his favourite composers were Mozart, Haydn and Beethoven. Stern and dogmatic individual that he was, he allied himself with the conservative factions in the music of the day as represented by Mendelssohn, Schumann and Brahms. He was strongly against the radical composer Liszt and loathed Wagner's music, although it was a point of honour with him to play Wagner's horn parts as well as possible and it was Franz Strauss who Wagner consulted about the big horn call in *Siegfried*. In spite of this, Wagner said 'This Strauss is a detestable fellow, but when he plays the horn one cannot be angry with him.' Franz gave the following advice to his son Richard when he was 18. 'It is ugly to move like a snake in the grass, particularly for a tall man like you. The fire of conducting comes from a different point. The left hand has to do nothing else but to turn the pages of the score, or, if there is no score, to keep still. Musicians are stimulated by the conductor's baton and eye. Please, dear Richard, follow my advice and stop these antics. You do not need to.'

In 1871 Franz Strauss was appointed professor at the Academy of Music in Munich and in 1873 a *Kammermusiker* by King Leopold II; he was later awarded the Ludwig Medal for Science and Art. He was a most serious teacher, though he never accepted a fee from his students. In 1875 he was elected conductor of an amateur orchestra in Vienna called the *Wilde Gung'l* and remained with them until 1895.

Friedrich Adolph Gumbert and early imports to the USA

Although not known outside the world of horn players, Friedrich Adolf Gumbert (1841–1906) remains a name of importance. He was the first horn with the Leipzig Gewandhaus Orchestra and professor at the Leipzig Conservatory from 1864 to 1898. His twelve volumes of orchestral studies are still 'standard issue' for all horn players, and he helped Kruspe to design the first double horn. His name was properly spelt with a *p* – Gumpert; but because there was reputedly a popular singer at the time called Gumbert the horn player's name was generally misspelt, and he presumably found it easier to tolerate the inaccuracy. Gumbert's influence as a teacher extended well beyond Leipzig and many of his students made names for themselves in the United States and Great Britain.

Anton Horner. Three of them were to have a major effect on horn playing in the USA. Each was born within a year of the others and the best remembered is Anton Horner (1877–1971), born at Grossengrün in Austria. His family emigrated to America when he was eight and lived in Philadelphia; his father was a violinist and Anton studied the same instrument from eight to thirteen. After his father died in 1890 the family returned to Europe, and a year later Anton was admitted into the Royal Music Conservatory in Leipzig as a violin student, learning the horn only as a second study. Friedrich Gumbert recognized his outstanding talent and persuaded him to study the horn as his first subject. After graduating in 1894 he returned to Philadelphia, and in 1899 was appointed first horn in the Pittsburg Symphony Orchestra under Victor Herbert.

At that time he changed from a single F horn by Schmidt to a Kruspe double horn, and for the next forty years he was the importer of Kruspe horns for the USA; he even designed one model, known as the 'Horner Model'. He played two summer seasons and one European tour with Sousa's band and in 1902 was appointed first horn with the Philadelphia Orchestra. He appeared only occasionally as a soloist and is best remembered as an orchestral player and teacher; he taught at the Curtis Institute of Music in Philadelphia from its founding in 1924 until 1942, and published *Primary Studies for the French Horn* in 1939. His style was heroic but with a wonderful lightness and buoyancy, as his recording of the *Siegfried* call made in 1912 shows most clearly.

Max Pottag. The second of these Gumbert pupils was Max Pottag (1876–1970), who was born in Forst in eastern Germany. He studied the violin and trumpet before taking up the horn at the age of fifteen. He entered the Royal Conservatory in Leipzig when he was 23, studying with Gumbert until he graduated with honours two years later. After a period with the Hamburg Symphony Orchestra as first horn he emigrated to the USA and in 1907 joined the Chicago Symphony Orchestra, where he remained for forty years, thirty-seven as second horn and three as fourth. He taught at North West University until 1952, made many arrangements for horn and compiled volumes of orchestral excerpts.

Max Hess. The third of Gumbert's students to go to the United States was Max Hess (1878–1975). Born at Klingenthal, in Saxony, he was the eldest son, and his father intended him to follow him into the family manufacturing business, but he went instead to the Royal Conservatory in Leipzig at the age of eighteen and on graduation three years later went immediately to the Rostock Opera as first horn, and a year later as first horn at the Frankfurt Opera. Again a year later he went to Cologne as teacher at the Hochschule and first horn with the Gürzenich Orchestra in Cologne, where he played in the first performance of Mahler's Fifth Symphony, with the composer conducting, in 1904. In 1905 he was offered the position of first horn in the Queen's Hall Orchestra in London and a similar position with the Boston Symphony. He chose Boston, where he remained as first horn for eight years before moving down to the third horn position because of an accident to his front teeth. In 1925, after having his teeth repaired, he went to the Cincinnati Orchestra as first horn under Fritz Reiner, returning to Boston after thirteen years on his retirement. He played a single F Bopp and later a five-valve B♭ Schmidt.

Other European players in the United States. It was not only from Germany that the United States imported its horn-players. Willem A. Valkenier was born in 1887 in Rotterdam and trained there. After playing in Johann Strauss's orchestra in Vienna and in various other orchestras in Holland, Austria and Germany he moved to Boston in 1923, where he remained as first horn until his retirement in 1950. He was a great influence as a player and taught at the New England Conservatory from 1936 to 1958. His first instrument was a single F Kessel, made in Holland; later he used another single F horn made by Slot. In America he used a double Kruspe and a double Schmidt.

Bruno Jaenicke (1887–1946), first horn in the New York Philharmonic, was originally from Potsdam, and Louis Dufresne (1878–1941), of the Chicago Symphony Orchestra, from Belgium. Alfred Brain (the elder son of A. E. Brain, the fourth horn in the London Symphony Orchestra when it was formed in 1904) was an exceptionally fine player who was for many years principal horn in the Queen's Hall Orchestra. He went to New York in 1923 to play with Walter Damrosch and later continued his career in Hollywood, adopting American nationality.

Horn playing in Great Britain

The high standard of horn playing in Britain was continued when a young German came to England to play first horn in Sir Henry Wood's Queen's Hall Orchestra. His name was Friedrich Adolf Borsdorf; he was born at Dittmansdorf, Saxony, in 1854 and studied at the Dresden Conservatory under Oscar Franz (the ultimate dedicatee of Richard Strauss's First Horn Concerto). He was by all accounts a magnificent player and musician; his breath control, phrasing and dynamic range were particularly admired, and he revolutionized horn teaching in Britain, which was said to have been in a bad way. In 1904, together with over forty of his colleagues, he resigned from the Queen's Hall Orchestra and helped to found the London Symphony Orchestra. The original horn section of the

LSO, of which he was principal, was a remarkable group of players and maintained such a high standard that it became known as 'God's own quartet'. Adolf Borsdorf played on a Raoux French horn built in 1821 for Giovanni Puzzi. He was horn professor at the Royal College of Music from 1882 and the Royal Academy of Music from 1897, remaining in both positions until his death in 1923. Among his students were the brothers Alfred and Aubrey Brain and Frank Probyn, who was Beecham's fourth horn for over a quarter of a century and who succeeded Borsdorf at the Royal College of Music. Two of his three sons, Emil and Oskar Francis, became horn players, the latter changing his name during the First World War to Francis Bradley. Bradley played with Sir Thomas Beecham for many years in the London Philharmonic Orchestra as third horn and later as first horn. From the LPO he moved to the Royal Opera House, Covent Garden, and recently retired as principal horn with the English National Opera.

Another German player who had a great influence in Britain was Franz Friedrich Paersch. He was born three years later than Adolf Borsdorf, at Thalheim, near Halle, and studied in Leipzig with Friedrich Gumbert. Paersch came to England in 1882, and his first engagement was with the summer orchestra at Buxton Spa, Derbyshire (which was the author's first engagement in England, sixty-nine years later). He moved on to Manchester, where he played first horn with the Halle Orchestra from 1883 to 1915 and taught the horn at the Royal Manchester College of Music. Franz Paersch's tone was superb, and he was apparently fantastically accurate and is said never to have missed a note. *The Spectator*, in reviewing a Leeds Festival, spoke of one phrase played by Mr Paersch as the most memorable experience of the Festival. Paersch also played much chamber music with many world-famous pianists and violinists – all this on an old Raoux French horn, which he used until it wore out, changing then to a French type horn made in London by W. Brown and Sons. He died in 1921 and was survived by his son Otto, who played the horn with the BBC Northern Orchestra until 1953.

The fourth horn in 'God's own quartet' was A. E. Brain, who had two horn playing sons, both pupils of Borsdorf. Alfred, the elder, as we have seen, went to America. His second son was the legendary Aubrey Brain, who after studying with Borsdorf was appointed principal horn with the New Symphony Orchestra at the age of eighteen. In 1932 he went as principal horn to the BBC Symphony Orchestra and remained there until his retirement in 1945. Aubrey Brain was also a great teacher and succeeded Borsdorf as horn professor at the Royal Academy of Music, remaining there until his death in 1955. He used a French horn in F and insisted that the rest of the BBC horn section should follow suit. He was a remarkable player, a supreme artist and an influence on all horn players.

Outstanding among Aubrey Brain's many distinguished pupils was his second son, Dennis Brain. He studied the horn at the Royal Academy of Music, and was also a fine organist. He left the Royal Academy during the Second World War and became, like many of the country's leading musicians, a member of the RAF Central Band at Uxbridge. It wasn't long before he was playing concertos throughout the country in his blue Royal Air Force uniform and his popularity and success were immediate. He played as first horn in the Royal Philharmonic and Philharmonia Orchestras, but he won fame mainly as a soloist and in chamber music; works specially written for him include Britten's *Serenade for Tenor, Horn and Orchestra*. His death in a motor accident at the age of 36 deprived the world of an exceptional musician. Dennis Brain was a phenomenon, and although he rarely gave lessons, his influence was enormous throughout the world and his example set standards of accuracy and facility that are difficult to approach.

At first Dennis Brain followed in his father's footsteps and played on a Raoux French horn, using an F crook, but the increasing demands of the heavy orchestral literature led him to modify his instrument by using a B♭ crook, and later he changed to a German horn, an Alexander in B♭.

Reginald F. Morley-Pegge (1890–1972) is an important name in the horn playing world, less as a player (most of his playing career was spent in France) than as a writer and historian of his instrument; his book *The French Horn* is the finest and most scholarly of text-books written. Morley-Pegge was born in London and educated at Summerfields and Harrow, where he played in the school orchestra. He went on to study in France and after a short period back in England returned to Paris at the age of 21 and enrolled at the Conservatoire. There he studied with François Brémond, a remarkable teacher who, being left-handed, tried with predictable unsuccess to teach his pupils to play with the left hand in the bell. Morley-Pegge also studied hand horn with Vuillermoz, as well as conducting. He played first with the Orchestre Symphonique de Paris, later with the Colonne Orchestra, the Paris Radio Orchestra and the Association de Concerts Pasdeloup. Returning to Britain during the Second World War, he played with the Reid Orchestra in Edinburgh.

While in Paris Morley-Pegge re-catalogued the wind instruments at the Conservatoire, and he acquired through the years one of the finest and most comprehensive collections of horns and other brass instruments, most of which are now housed with the Philip Bate Collection at the Oxford University Faculty of Music.

National schools of horn playing

Dennis Brain's switch from a French to a German horn was a sign of the times. Various national styles of horn playing had developed over the years; the lineage of the horn's evolution began with the French *cor de chasse* bands and led directly to the Bohemian school, from which developed the two distinctive styles of Germany and France. Up to the mid-twentieth century horn styles were distinctive, and it was relatively easy to detect the nationality of a player. The French had a light tone and a pronounced *vibrato*; the Germans a thick, dark sound with no *vibrato*; the English a pure, thinner quality, again without *vibrato*. During the evolution of the horn the bell became much wider so that the player was better able to use the hand horn technique, and that was one of the reasons for the darker, richer sound in Central Europe. France and England resisted the Viennese type instrument and continued to play on the smaller bored instrument with a narrow throated bell. Feelings ran high on the subject, and still do for that matter. The strong national opinion in England as to how the horn should sound was clearly set out by Cecil Forsyth in his book *Orchestration*, first published in 1914:

In France the instrument is often built in B♭ alto. This is much less satisfactory than the medium-pitched key of F. Crooks have to be continuously used and, even when the tuning slides are pulled out, the piston-notes on the lower crooks are all far too sharp. In Germany G is a favourite key for the manufacture of valve-horns. The German instruments have very little resemblance to our own. Their tone-quality we should regard as more suitable to the euphonium. It is somewhat coarse, thick and 'open'. In lightness and brilliance they are inferior to the true French horns. The explanation is to be found in the bore and mouthpiece of the German instruments. It must be added that they are much easier to play. Both tonal and executive control seem to be acquired without much difficulty. The Germans appear to be unaware of the instrument's deficiencies both in elegance and lightness. This is perhaps mainly a matter of custom, though it is surprising that in America some of the finest orchestras should deliberately prefer German to French or English players.

Things have changed now, not least because much of the music written for horn players by modern composers is simply unplayable on the narrow-bored French horn in F. When Borsdorf and Paersch came to England, they changed to the French horn, and as already noted Aubrey Brain would have no other to play beside him; but Dennis

Brain finally exchanged his French Raoux for a German Alexander. However, there have been many other cross-overs. Many Germans now play with a much lighter sound and use a *vibrato*, while many French players have adopted the characteristics associated with the German school and the *vibrato* is not so popular. The English school has similarly been contaminated and the sound is in some cases now darker than dark. It is frequently assumed that it has been in part due to the use of the wide-bore German-type instruments, but this is not entirely so. The horn playing on recordings made by the London Philharmonic Orchestra in the 1930s with Sir Thomas Beecham is extremely English, but this section, led by Charles Gregory, used wide-bore Alexander horns.

Russian playing is often confused with that of their French colleagues because of their use of *vibrato*, but closer examination will show that they have a much darker sound and use a wider vibrato. Players in eastern Europe have copied the Russian style to some extent and it is sometimes very difficult to tell them apart. The one exception is the playing in Czechoslovakia; the Bohemians continue today to be the most romantic of all and retain the true, rich colour of the Bohemian school, particularly the players from Brno.

The Viennese, too, in particular those who play with the Vienna State Opera and Philharmonic Orchestra, try to preserve their easily identifiable sound; they still use the old Viennna horn with the F terminal crook and the Vienna valves for about 90 per cent of the time. In the other 10 per cent they use a B♭ alto crook and sometimes a rotary-valved F alto instrument.

In the United States horn tone has become something of an amalgam. This reflects the immigration patterns. Anton Horner, Max Pottag and Max Hess, who all came from Leipzig, brought with them the darker German sound. Dufresne hailed from Belgium and imported a lighter sound. Each man had his pupils and his own sphere of special influence, and horn colours in American orchestras tended to differ accordingly. Horner's field was on the east coast, especially around Philadelphia; Dufresne's in the Middle West, around Chicago. Horn sounds therefore differ across the continent, but, as in Europe, the cross-over of styles has changed in recent years and it is not so easy now to identify individual orchestras, the exceptions being the Philadelphia Orchestra and the New York Philharmonic, who still continue to play with a markedly darker sound than the rest of their American colleagues.

Five

Building the Horn – a Transposing Instrument

The earliest metal instruments were made from sheets of copper or brass, hammered and folded over a wooden shape or mandril, then brazed into a single piece to form a tube, which was filled with molten lead. This was allowed to cool, and the tube was bent into a curved shape; the lead was then melted again so that it could be extracted. When the horn was made longer it was built in sections joined together to make the hoop-shaped instrument with which we are familiar today. Present-day manufacture does not greatly differ from this process; the conical sections are still formed over a mandril, now made of hardened steel, and many of the cylindrical parts are made with hydraulic machines which expand the metal tube inside a mould. The narrower conical sections, the mouthpipe and the first branch after the valve section, used to be made by forcing a cylinder of brass tubing on to a shaped mandril. This was done by hand, the craftsman thrusting the tube and mandril through a piece of soft metal with a series of holes of diminishing diameter until the required shape was obtained.

The body of the horn

Nowadays the general process is usually done in a single stage using a machine. Most bells are now entirely spun from a flat disc of brass on to a series of mandrils of increasing proportions, and those made from sheet brass must still be spun in the final stages. All the spinning and bending of the tubing is done while the metal is cold, but the process changes the molecular structure of the metal, which becomes harder and harder until it is unworkable; it then has to be softened or annealed. This is done by heating the metal to a controlled high temperature and then allowing it to cool gradually, when it is ready for further working.

Brass instruments are still made in a very labour-intensive fashion, but much of the equipment used in manufacture has been developed so that a high degree of standardization is possible. In the first part of the twentieth century, when instruments were largely hand-built, many extraordinarily fine ones were produced, but a great many were defective, and a good instrument was a prized possession. With the increase in mass production a far higher number of mediocre horns is produced, but no really outstanding horns are built today by mass production.

The production line method cannot cater for individual needs, so that leading players are going more and more to a few craftsmen who are prepared to spend the long hours necessary to hand-craft the crucial sections such as the mouthpipe and the sections between the valves and the bell – the conical parts where the degree of taper will make or mar a horn. This can be very expensive, and it is mainly professionals who indulge in it. A horn costs much less than a bassoon, and when compared with a string instrument it is still a fairly cheap instrument to buy. On the other hand, brass instruments deteriorate with age; corrosion is a major factor and in addition the metal, which is extremely thin, is easily dented, and each time that happens the playing characteristics change. The metals from which horns are built vary in appearance from a dark copper colour to silver, but they are always basically brass – a mixture of copper and zinc. The different colours are due to the different proportions of the ingredients. Three basic alloys are used now: gold brass, which is about 80 per cent copper and 20 per cent zinc; yellow brass, about 70 per cent copper and 30 per cent zinc; and 'silver', which is an alloy, in varying proportions, of copper, zinc and nickel. Each has a different response – the more copper used, the darker the sound, and the more nickel, the lighter. An instrument made of pure copper looks very beautiful, but has a very dead quality when played. It used to be thought that silver horns made a dark sound; some Kruspes were made of silver and possessed such a sound, and the same metal was used for one of the most popular instruments ever made in America, the Conn 8D. But the darker sound was due, as has since been conclusively proved by acoustical tests, not to the metal used but to the wider throated bell.

Mouthpipe and mouthpiece

The horn can be divided into the following sections: mouthpiece, mouthpipe, valve section, bell section – all the tubing with the exception of the valve section being conical. It is the difference in diameter that gives the horn its distinctive tone. Other factors are the contours of the mouthpiece – funnel-shaped, unlike the other brass instruments, which use cup-shaped mouthpieces – and the extreme narrowness of the tube at the beginning.

Mouthpieces

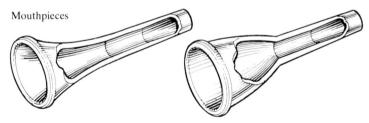

The first section of every brass instrument, the mouthpipe, is the most crucial; it is the degree of taper that dictates the behaviour of all the harmonics. One taper will favour the high register and another the low, and the care taken in building the mouthpipe is of the utmost importance. Similarly, the mouthpiece must be made very carefully. Early mouthpieces were made from a sheet of brass, but today they are turned on a lathe from a solid piece of metal, a more accurate process.

The rim of the horn mouthpiece is usually much narrower than that of other brass instruments. In recent years experiments have been made with a wide rimmed mouthpiece, but it has not yet found widespread favour. The characteristic funnel shape has also been tampered with; a slight cup or quick narrowing of the inner shape has been introduced into some mouthpieces to assist in more precise attack in the high register, but this causes a decided change in the tone and is not universally popular. There is a short parallel section which leads to an expansion of the shape which is called the backbore; this is really the beginning of the horn proper, and a tight fit into the horn is crucial for optimum results.

Generally speaking, a large diameter mouthpiece will aid flexibility and is best for a player specializing in the middle and low registers, and a slight cup shape will assist the player in the highest register, but the final choice must be left to the player. Horn players change instruments from time to time, but tend to stick to the same mouthpiece, in some cases throughout their playing careers. It becomes a part of them, so to speak, and they become so used to its characteristics that a change is unthinkable. On the other hand, most players have gone through at least one stage of experimentation, usually early in their careers, in search of the 'perfect' mouthpiece; but in the end they are faced with the stark realization that it is the player himself who controls the instrument. He does so through the mouthpiece, which must be his servant. There is no perfect mouthpiece, and the orthodox mouthpiece is always preferable to one that will assist a player to overcome certain weaknesses in his technique.

A student is well advised to use a proven, standard, conventional mouthpiece and stick to it. The design is the result of many hundreds of years' evolution, and it would be surprising if anything drastically new were to appear.

Mutes

Efforts were being made to alter the sound of the horn in the mid-eighteenth century, and it was those experiments with putting objects into the bell that led, not only to the mute, but also, more important, to the art of hand-horn playing.

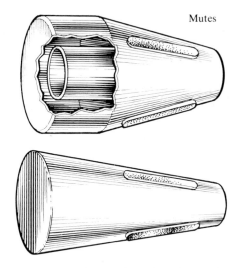

Mutes

The mute generally used today is made of fibre or cardboard, with a base usually of wood or some solid substance, and it is built in one of two basic shapes.

Only horn mutes have a cylinder built inside. Its purpose is to lower the pitch, which otherwise becomes too sharp. Narrow strips of cork are glued along the side to serve as a means of keeping the mute fixed in the bell.

A transposing mute

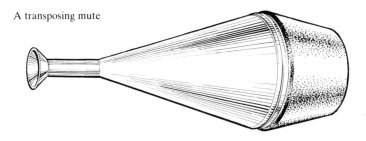

The only other type of mute in current use is the transposing mute. It is made of metal, and when put into the bell changes the pitch as well as the sound. For this reason it is all too often thought of as a substitute for hand stopping, and although the sound produced is similar it is not the same, and should be used with discretion.

Paul Hindemith was a master of the orchestra and possessed an almost unequalled knowledge of each instrument. He is said to have been able to play every instrument in the orchestra, so it is curious that he should have written such a conflicting instruction as he did in his Horn Concerto. The player is asked to do the impossible: play muted and hand-stopped at the same time!

The horn is still a transposing instrument

The first horn parts to be written down were rather primitive codes to denote basic rhythms. When longer horns were built more harmonics were brought within the player's reach and conventional musical symbols began to be used. But the first horn-players were not trained musicians and it was found to be simpler to write horn music in C, where C denoted the tonic of the scale. In other words a written C would sound D on a D horn, E♭ on an E♭ horn, E on an E horn and so on, and since no modulation or chromatic playing was possible the system worked very well. This tradition continued when the horn joined the orchestra in concerted music to be played indoors, and many of the early players would have had difficulty in learning to read music chromatically.

Even when the horn was an accepted part of musical life

and trained musicians were playing it, the tradition pre-vailed. The horn parts of the classical period mostly use the open harmonics with occasional hand-stopped notes and rarely modulate very far from the tonic key, so the C-equals-tonic system is really easier both to write and to read. When the instrument had become fully chromatic the key of F was found for a time to be the best key in which to build a three valve horn, and consequently it became customary to write the music in F – that is, sounding a fifth lower than written. Horns pitched in other keys were used, of course, but most fell into disfavour apart from the B♭ alto and more recently, the F alto.

Apart from Brahms, who wanted all his horn parts to be played on natural horns (though they seldom if ever were), most composers conformed to writing horn parts in F. The notable exceptions, of course, were Wagner and Strauss, who, while using F as the basic key, changed to E for sharp keys and E♭ for flat keys, to obviate the use of accidentals. This method had its merits, though they took it to an impractical extreme by additionally writing in the bass clef. Horn parts in the classical period were mostly written in the treble clef, the only notes out of its range being the two lowest played notes, the second and third harmonics. Consequently, horn players are not generally adept in reading from the bass clef. For some curious reason these bass clef notes were written an octave lower, and this tradition prevailed right into the twentieth century; now-adays it is more usual to write the bass clef horn parts in the correct register.

By the time that composers were writing more elaborate passages for the chromatic horn, the F crook had become standard with the result that, while players were expert in reading chromatic passages in F, the other keys had to some extent been neglected. As players and conductors neglect their transposition more and more, some passages printed in their original notation, such as the third and fourth horn parts of the *Scherzo Capriccioso* by Dvořák, will trip up most players on first sight:

Horn

Allegro con fuoco
Hns. 3.4 (B♭ basso)

Italian composers largely stuck to writing valve horn parts in keys other than F, probably because players in Italy were still prepared to change their crooks and adjust their valve slides when asked; but the music modulates to such a small extent that it poses no special problems for expert players to keep their horn pitched in F and/or B♭ and transpose accordingly.

When Arnold Schoenberg wrote his Wind Quintet Op. 26 he wrote the clarinet and horn parts at concert pitch, but the clarinet part, going down to C♯ concert, must clearly be played on an A and not a C clarinet. Horn passages like the following from this quintet illustrate the usual impracticability of writing horn parts at concert pitch:

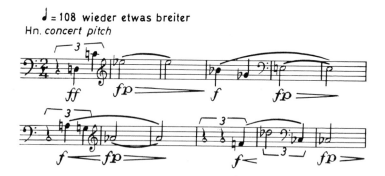

♩ = 108 wieder etwas breiter
Hn. concert pitch

If the passage is written for the horn in F it all lies conveniently on the treble stave:

When the Wind Quintet was first published the clarinet and horn parts were printed as they appeared in the score, in C, but that proved so confusing that they had to be reprinted in A and F respectively. More and more composers nowadays are writing transposing instruments at concert pitch, but it is for their own benefit and should not be thought of as an aid to conductors, who should be fully conversant with the basic transpositions. These C-pitch scores still have to use the alto and tenor clefs for bassoon, trombone, viola and cello parts, so the advantages are arguably only marginal.

Six
Advice for Beginners

Parents of aspiring horn players frequently ask what is the best age for a child to begin to learn. The decision must rest on two factors: physical size and mental development. The first point is obvious, as the horn is quite awkward to hold for a small person, and a child should not start to learn it until he can reach inside the bell with his right hand. Right hand technique is not just an adjunct to horn playing; it is part and parcel of it. It must also be born in mind that the player must be able to cope with the physical exertion of the face muscles and abdomen needed to play the horn. It is probably better to start on some smaller instrument – trumpet, cornet or E♭ tenor horn – to develop the basic technique of brass playing, and then to change to the horn with developing physical maturity.

The second point is more difficult to define. The young boy or girl may tend to play too much by instinct and develop bad habits that can become so well ingrained as to be incurable later on. Instinctive playing is as wrong for the adult as it is for the young beginner. The horn player must have a split personality; he must have a warm heart, but it is essential to combine it with a cool head. One half of his mind tells him how a piece, a phrase, even a single note should be played, while the other half constantly analyses his physical condition, the degree of fatigue in his face muscles, the amount of usable breath left in the lungs, the pitch of the instrument, the relative intonation of other players, the amount of water in the horn and in which bends it is situated, the behaviour of the instrument on a particular note – whether it is a good or a defective harmonic. All these things and many more are what a player has to think about during a performance.

A reasonable degree of mental as well as physical development is therefore necessary before embarking on any serious training on the horn, and this stage is usually reached around the age of thirteen.

Buying an instrument

Once the decision is made to learn the horn the next step is to acquire an instrument. The best course of action is to consult a good player, who will be able to give advice and test any instrument – a good retailer will always agree to let instruments be taken away and tested. However, the would-be hornist may not know any experienced player and in this case he must exercise the utmost caution. If the potential purchase is a brand new instrument, then it is presumed that the valves will be in first-class working order, that the instrument will be free from dents and that some sort of guarantee will accompany it. Even with these basics taken care of, it is advisable to buy a horn that will have a good resale value. There are good and bad makes of professional and student's models, so it is advisable to stick to a well known make that will command a reasonable price should the horn ever be re-sold.

If a second-hand horn is being considered, there are three basic things to look for. First of all, brass instruments are easily dented. Dents can be removed, but the metal deteriorates each time it is bent and straightened, and even though it may appear to be in good order, care should be taken to examine the bell area and the tubing for any evidence of previous damage. The bell dictates the tone of the instrument, and frequent bending will destroy its qualities to a point at which the instrument is of little value. Dents and signs of earlier mistreatment should be looked for elsewhere, of course, but the two areas mentioned are the most crucial and the most likely to be damaged.

Secondly, loose braces are an indication of neglect, and a horn that is virtually falling apart should be avoided. Lastly, the valves should be carefully examined for signs of excessive wear. They can be rebuilt, but this is an extremely expensive operation and should only be entrusted to a first-class repair man. Each valve should be tested individually; the easiest method is to remove a slide, press down the valve lever and blow through the horn while covering the end of the open slide with a finger. All valves leak to some extent; but if there is any excessive wear, air will be heard escaping round the valve itself. If this happens second thoughts should be given about the instrument.

With a rotary valve, find out if there is too much end play. To do this, hold one end of the rotor and try to move it up and down. End play is not as serious as leakage, but it can cause valves to stick and will certainly make them noisy. Leaky valves can cause an otherwise excellent horn to perform poorly, but by flooding the rotor with a thick mineral oil such as is used to lubricate sewing machines a good seal can be obtained. It will make the valves very sluggish, of course, but it will show whether or not the horn would play well if repaired.

Badly peeling lacquer can be unsightly, while not affecting the playing characteristics of the horn, but it is expensive to have the instrument cleaned and relacquered. If the horn has turned green, or almost black, but still performs well, it will only be a matter of expending a lot of elbow grease cleaning it with metal polish. Many players feel that lacquer has a detrimental effect on horns, but there is no clear evidence to prove it. A positive advantage is that good lacquer protects the instrument from external corrosion.

The first instrument

The beginner should start to learn on the F horn, since it has a good basic tone and provides a greater number of harmonics within the player's range; as a result the student will develop a more conscious awareness of embouchure control than if he starts on a B♭ horn. There are many very good three-valve rotary horns available that will help to give the serious student, or the amateur, a good understanding of the instrument and a solid grounding in basic technique. When a reasonable standard of proficiency is achieved a move should be made to the double horn in F and B♭.

The B♭ horn has a completely different response from the F horn, and its tone can be very rough in the middle register. The best way to learn it is to practise the same exercises that were used on the F horn. When the student is familiar with both sides of the horn, he can play the instrument chomatically.

Maintenance and repair

Great care should be taken to avoid denting the horn. It is a fragile musical instrument, very easily damaged by accident or through neglect. The best policy is always to return it to its case when not in use. Because of its awkward, asymmetrical shape it easily falls over and should never be placed on a chair or near the edge of a table. A case rarely affords complete protection, so it too should be kept in a safe position, preferably on the ground. Even a small, seemingly insignificant dent can twist the tubing and put a great strain on the whole horn, resulting in distortions of the valve casing which can in extreme circumstances cause a complete seizing up of the rotor, something that can be dealt with only by an expert repair man.

Maintaining the horn, however, is a very simple matter, basically a matter of frequent and generous lubrication. There are many expensive lubricants and greases available, but underneath all the fancy packaging they are petroleum products of varying consistencies. Many have silicon additives (these should be avoided) and some contain deodorants to counter the strong smell of kerosene. The following grades of lubricant are recommended: a very fine one for the inside of the valves and the end bearings of the rotors, a thicker oil for the key mechanism and springs and a much thicker grease for the slides. Whatever the outside packaging may say, the fine lubricant is usually kerosene, and it can be more economically purchased from a hardware store. The best oil for the key mechanism is a pure mineral oil such as is used for lubricating sewing machines. The slides require a much thicker substance such as axlegrease. All three of these substances are petroleum-based and are well proven lubricants for metal surfaces. Moreover, as they will inevitably mix together there will be no conflict between them. If they are used once a day, or whenever the horn is played, there will be only imperceptible wear on the bearings and corrosion will be kept in check. Anything containing animal fat, such as lanolin, should be avoided.

Playing technique

All musical sounds are made up of different harmonics. The harmonic series is comparable with the colour spectrum and follows a precise mathematical pattern. A column of air agitated in a tube, by vibration either of the lips or of a reed, by blowing against an edge as in the flute, will vibrate. Every tube has a harmonic series and this subject is treated more fully in the Introduction (pp. xix–xxi).

How the sound is made. One of the most exciting moments in a horn player's life is when he produces his first sound on the horn. For some people it happens without a great deal of effort; others have to go to a lot of trouble before the instrument roars into life. The initial success or failure doesn't necessarily have any bearing on a player's later proficiency, though it is obviously more gratifying to make a sound at the first attempt. The most common way to do this is to take a breath, purse the lips and blow a raspberry into the horn, and although this is only a rough guide to the way one should start to play it is enough to start the new player on a course of instruction. The new horn player with his first horn will clearly need more precise information, and a good teacher is the best person to provide this, but if none is immediately available, the beginner should use one of the printed methods of instruction which treat each aspect of playing technique in great detail. This book is not primarily devoted to instruction, but it would be inappropriate to neglect the rudiments of playing, and the following summary is intended to enlighten the non-player and to encourage the new player. Some aspects of playing are dealt with more fully from the point of view of the teacher in Chapter Eight.

The formation of the lips is called the embouchure. Generally it involves closing the lips not too firmly and placing two thirds of the mouthpiece on the upper lip and one third on the lower. An older method, known as the *Einsetzen* or inset embouchure, in which the player actually digs the mouthpiece into the red part of the lower lip, has largely gone out of fashion, but its validity as a way of playing can be supported by the fact that Aubrey Brain and his son Dennis both used it. The precise positioning of the lips is best left between teacher and pupil, for the exact use of the lips in playing is a very subtle art. Generalizations can be dangerous, and often indeed misleading, and the new player is advised again to find the best available teacher and to read the specialized books published on the subject.

Breathing. The lips placed together and against the mouthpiece will not create a sound in themselves and must be activated by the breath to make the air column inside the horn vibrate. Neither breathing nor embouchure can function without the other and breathing could be likened to the bow of a violin moving across the strings. It is the juxtaposition of breath pressure and lip tension that dictates not only what note is produced but the dynamic and quality of the sound. Just how practised one must be in the art of breathing can be easily demonstrated by asking a layman to blow up a balloon; instinctively he will take a great gulp of air and blow with all his might, perhaps even blowing out his cheeks, and in a few seconds he will be out of breath. The mistake he has made is to breathe only from his chest. To perfect extensive breath control it is necessary to understand that the lungs in themselves are not particularly powerful, and that it is essential to use all the supporting muscles. First of all, extra room must be made for the lungs to expand, as the rib cage expands only a little. To do this the abdominal muscles must be distended so that the diaphragm, underneath the lungs, will be able to move downwards.

Exhaling is not such a problem; it is the prevention of it that requires practice. The body instinctively tries to rid the lungs of stale air, and in normal circumstances the breathing cycle is completed by breathing out without any conscious effort. Right from birth this cycle begins with a demand for oxygen. The baby begins its life away from the mother without having previously used its lungs and in most cases takes its first breath instinctively. It is important to note that under normal conditions the breath is never held; instead, exhalation takes place as soon as sufficient breath is taken to supply the blood stream with oxygen. The air in the lungs deteriorates rapidly and must be got rid of. When that is done there is a momentary pause, sometimes of several seconds, before the process begins again. The most difficult part of breathing is the controlled use of exhalation; but before describing this in detail, the controlled as opposed to the instinctive taking of breath should be analysed.

Most people over-breathe at first by taking more breath than they need. Ideally the player should take only enough breath to play the intended note or phrase, so that when it is finished the lungs are fully rid of air. If that is not done, air is left over in the lungs which has to be exhaled before the next inhalation, and this produces many problems of endurance. First of all, it must be understood that chest expansion is limited, so that if the lungs are to be expanded fully space must be made for them by extending the abdomen so that the diaphragm moves downwards to give the lungs this additional room.

Many players hold their breath momentarily before exhaling, but there are several good reasons for *not* doing this. In this first place, it is inefficient because the oxygen deteriorates as soon as it is taken into the lungs, and even a split second of unnecessary delay wastes what may be a valuable quantity of breath. Any constriction of the throat to prevent the breath from leaving the body uses extra physical energy, and this in turn burns up the oxygen in the lungs. Holding the breath also implies a building up of pressure, and this leads to additional complications. Each given note at a given dynamic requires a certain embouchure setting and breath pressure, and it is difficult to start the note if a greater pressure is built up in the lungs than is required. It is more logical and efficient, therefore, to inhale to a point where only the required amount of air has been taken in and then immediately and swiftly to constrict the abdomen until there is sufficient air pressure to start the note.

All this should be done quickly in one continuous movement, without any pause. When we speak we give little or no attention to how we breathe, and a lot can be learnt from a simple experiment: to count aloud at one second intervals – 'one' (pause), 'two' (pause), 'three' (pause), 'four' (pause), 'five' (pause) and so on – and to pay attention to the instinctive behaviour of the body. To begin with, there is preparatory inhalation and an immediate exhalation to actuate the vocal cords with no hesitation. Once the first number has been spoken there is a momentary pause during which the breathing is arrested, but not by constricting the throat which will result in a build-up of air pressure. Of course, more air pressure is needed to play the horn than for talking, but this same principle can be applied to wind playing as a basis for breathing technique. Players tend to complicate their way of preventing exhalation and a careful analysis of how the breath is controlled during speech is of great benefit.

Posture. If the student sits and/or stands in a defective way his technique will be hampered throughout his playing life. It is therefore essential to cultivate a comfortable and efficient position for both standing and sitting. Students can quite rightly refer to an outstanding player who, despite his dreadful posture, is able to perform well. The answer to this is that this player, if he could correct his posture, would be able to play even better. Also it must be remembered that youth usually possesses an excess of energy that can, for a time, override the physical limitations of bad posture and that the real problems will arise when the player is over thirty. Whether standing or sitting, the player should hold his body in an efficient way, allowing the lungs to expand without hindrance. When sitting the feet should be placed apart, firmly on the ground and the legs should never be crossed. A support to the lower part of the back is a great help, but slumping into a chair will only detract from optimum efficiency.

Holding the horn. There are two ways of holding the horn. One is to rest the bell on the thigh, the other is to hold it free, supporting the entire weight with the hands. Each has its strong adherents, but holding the horn free gives a far greater physical freedom and prevents the player from slumping over the horn. To do this, the right hand position must not only support the horn comfortably but must also be flexible. The hand should be held in a scoop shape with the fingers and thumb together, so that the horn rests mostly on the thumb and index finger, the other fingers resting along the side of the bell farthest from the body.

It is then fairly simple to bring the palm across the bell to close it fully. To prevent the mouthpiece from being bumped away from the embouchure when hand stopping,

Horn

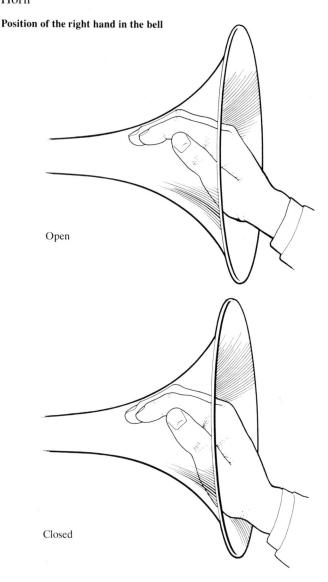

Open

Closed

the rim of the bell can be rested against the rib cage. If the player wishes to play standing up the horn can be held in the same way, and the standing position for solo playing gives the player an advantage both acoustically and psychologically.

Tonguing. Making a controlled start to the sound with the tongue is called 'tonguing'. It is customary to articulate each note by withdrawing the tongue quickly from the hard palate at the same time as breathing out – very much, though not exactly, as when one says 'tee', 'dee' or 'nee'.

It is not absolutely necessary to use the tongue to begin a sound, but it does enable a player to start a note with more precision. A player can get a better understanding of the synchronization and control of tonguing and breathing by not using the tongue at all, and although this is not the most efficient way of starting notes it can help to prevent an over-dependence on the tongue, which should be thought of as an aid to the embouchure and breathing, not the prime initiator of the notes. Nothing should be done automatically or instinctively; every action should be well thought out and premeditated; only then will the player be able to approach the ideal state when the horn is a servant to his musical expression.

When very rapid articulation is called for it may be necessary to use what is called double tonguing and triple tonguing. Double tonguing is no more than alternating the 'te' sound with a 'ke' sound, so that the tongue is used in a rocking fashion. This is not so easy to do when playing and the sound may be uneven to begin with, quite a lot of practice is needed to make the sounds equal. Triple tonguing uses the same technique for triplet figures, with three possible articulations: '*te*-te-ke-*te*-te-ke' etc., '*te*-ke-te-*te*-ke-te' etc. or '*te*-ke-te-*ke*-te-ke' etc. The third of these is of course basically double tonguing with a stress made on each third sound.

Trills. A different embouchure and breath pressure is necessary for each note, and in a trill this rapid alternation is a difficult technique to master. Half-tone trills can be played using the valves, but even these will sound more impressive using the lips and breath alone. A better, if more cumbersome, term would be lip and breath trills. For whole tone trills it is possible to use the valves in the lower register, but above middle C concert they are of little help because of the closer proximity of the harmonics and they do not sound as well. So the use of lips and breath must be developed. Such trills can sound very impressive and are always a feature of works composed in the classical period. Consequently the lip trill is an inherent part of horn playing and must be practised assiduously by all players.

Hand technique. If the horn is held correctly, without tension, both hands will be able to perform their functions properly. If the arms are bent so that the forearms are almost vertical there will be less strain on the arm muscles.

It is important that the hook for the little finger is positioned so that the other fingers will rest over the valve keys; this hook may have to be moved by a repair man, and *should* be if it is badly placed. When the valve keys are pressed care must be taken to keep the fingers rounded and not to let the first joint bend the wrong way as it is unsightly and inefficient. It is the right hand technique which is an essential of good horn playing. Only trial and error will determine the best basic position, but the principle must be that the player should use a position which will enable him to play the instrument as a hand horn. The hand put carelessly into the bell can positively hinder intonation and tone, and it should be used so that it will complement the valves, as there is no valve system yet devised that is 'in tune'. The right hand can assist the embouchure in correcting intonation as well as helping the player to vary his sound. To do this the hand should be placed in the bell so that the outside of the fingers rest flush to the bell as far as is desired, allowing the player to open the bell to sharpen notes or to close it to lower the pitch or to 'stop' the horn. The best way for a student to cultivate a constant awareness to the possibilities of hand-horn technique is to learn how to play all pre-valve horn music without valves; this has the added benefit of helping to strengthen the embouchure. A proficient hand-horn player will be a better valve-horn player.

Seven
The Horn Player, Artist and Technician

Though there are of course opportunities for solo and chamber music playing, a horn player's life will necessarily revolve round the orchestra. The classical distinction between first and second horns, cors alto and cors basse, has long since disappeared; every player is now expected to be capable of playing over the whole of the instrument's range, though both temperament and actual physical characteristics may tend to give individuals a preference for the higher or the lower parts. Horn players in the orchestra are still divided into pairs, one high and one low, so that the third horn is still the first horn of the second pair.

Many aspiring students, and amateurs, want to play first horn because they feel that other positions are of less importance. This is quite wrong, except of course that the first player has more solos to play. All positions are interesting and each has its own responsibilities. The second horn has one of the most difficult parts, frequently being required to play as high as the first horn and then to jump down to the lower register. The acrobatic side of his playing is generally unknown even to his close colleagues – unless of course they too have played second horn.

The third horn, as the first horn of the second pair, has a very nice time, particularly in Brahms, where he is given nearly as many solos as the principal, but with a much lighter work load. It is the third and fourth horns who introduce the slow movement of Brahms's Fourth Symphony:

Richard Strauss gives his famous *Till Eulenspiegel* call to the third horn as well as to the first, but played a third lower, in D major:

The fourth horn plays less than the other three and is rarely asked to play in a high register, but his role as the bass of the horn section is of great importance. Apart from being the second horn of the second pair, he has some well known solos: well known, that is, to horn players, less so to others. Richard Strauss distributes his favours most generously through the horn section. The fourth horn joins the other three in the joyous motifs in *Don Juan*:

and also has a small solo for himself:

In *Don Quixote* there is a rather longer solo:

The horn section performs as a solo group at times. One of the earliest examples is in the Overture to Weber's *Der Freischütz*:

Horn

With so much glorious horn writing to choose from, it is interesting to examine some less well known passages. Sibelius gives the horn and bassoon sections an accompanying role in his Violin Concerto:

Sibelius uses the bassoon as a bass voice under the horn quartet. In the Overture to *Semiramide* Rossini also includes bassoons but – as in the case of Beethoven's 'Abscheulicher' (pp. 72–3) – they add chromatic harmony, because the horn was still in the pre-valve era:

Horn

174

'from the overture to *Semiramide*'

In the second act of *Götterdämmerung* Wagner gives the horns the following exciting section, in which first two, then four, then six, and finally eight horns contribute to the overall effect:

Horn

176

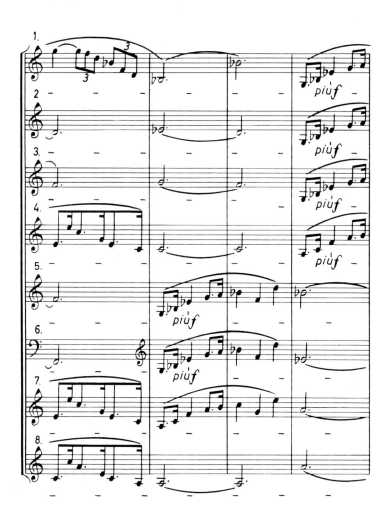

Horn

It would seem so elementary to stagger the breathing in long phrases that it is surprising that it is done so rarely, it is therefore important to single out Paul Hindemith, who shows quite specifically where the horns should breathe in the long melody in his Concert Music for Brass and Strings:

Fatigue

The ratio of physical exertion to artistic output is very lopsided for the horn player, and because fatigue is a major factor it is usual for composers to give the horns a lot of time to rest. But it is the player's responsibility to strike a balance between the way he would like to play a particular passage and his assessment of his physical potential at that time. To ignore the constantly fluctuating strength of the delicate face muscles and the rapid change in the instrument's temperature, affecting both intonation and condensation, is to invite disaster. On the other hand, to play for safety, keeping well within the safety limits of the moment, is to produce boring and unmusical results. Both aspects must be kept under review by the player, and if he is prepared to take sensible risks, as opposed to foolish miscalculations, the composer's wishes will be served and the listener will be rewarded.

If the first horn might become over-tired in particularly testing pieces an assistant player is sometimes used to take some of the strain. Concert-goers are puzzled to see five horn players sitting in the orchestra to play a work in which the composer only asks for four. The fifth, sitting outside the first horn, is there to increase the volume in *fortissimo* passages and play occasional passages while the first horn recovers his strength.

Inside the orchestra

Orchestral playing calls for different abilities from each instrumentalist. The first horn has to combine being a section leader, lending support to the woodwind and brass sections and shining forth as a soloist when required. There are certain key figures in the orchestra on whom the conductor will rely and who are in charge of particular sections. The first flute and first oboe are obvious leaders of woodwind, both artistically and visually, but the importance of the first horn is a little less obvious. To begin with, he is seated at the back of the orchestra and is therefore only on view to the conductor. He does, however, wield a considerable amount of influence. Naturally the members of the horn section will look to him to set a style of playing, but he is also an important link between the woodwind and the brass sections. Since the horns spend most of their time playing with one or both of these groups in a supporting role the first horn must be quick to adapt to, say, the first trumpet or first clarinet both in style and in ensemble.

It is not always possible to rely completely on the conductor's beat – indeed, sometimes it is not even desirable, since beating time is not the prime consideration. The players within an orchestra have to develop a rapport amongst themselves so as to become an ensemble which if need be can play with no beat at all. An outstanding woodwind section can do this, and of course a horn section should be no less cohesive a group of musicians. The concert-goer is sometimes mystified by the apparent inattention of the musicians in the orchestra, who do not appear to be watching the conductor. The fact is that the work has been done at the rehearsals, the *tempi* and rubatos practised over and over again. In any case, the conductor is within each player's field of vision, who may not be looking directly at him; he is none the less aware of his arm movements and will be quick to watch more closely in emergencies or during awkward tempo changes.

The conductor frequently communicates with only one section or player, and that is when the experienced player will listen and follow. It is during rubatos that a good section leader can keep his section together while following the conductor, the melody line and other accompanying instruments.

When it comes to playing a solo or exposed passage, each player will have his individual conception of how it should go, which may be in direct conflict with the interpretation of the conductor. In such circumstances he must subordinate his own instincts and feelings to those of the conductor, but this can be very difficult to do. In a tricky technical passage, for instance, it may be necessary to change the breathing points to accommodate the conductor's interpretation, and the first time he plays in the new way he may not get it right. A first class instrumentalist can usually adjust very quickly, but a less experienced or less competent player will find it more difficult. Then, when the conductor pursues his point, the player may feel harassed, and play less well. Under these circumstances only experience and confidence will help.

Orchestral playing is not at all easy. Quite frequently it is impossible to hear what is going on and the player's own sound may be lost to him, such is the amount of sheer noise generated by the brass and percussion in a *fortissimo tutti* passage. Many auditoria and recording studios have an acoustic which makes the players from the opposite side of the platform sound late, and in such cases the orchestra player must know how to play with one eye on the beat. So the orchestral musician is no mere employee, but an executive who must exercise great personal responsibility.

Band playing

The horn is about the most awkward instrument there is to play on the march. A line of shining horns in the parade looks pretty, but the attraction is only visual, since the horn contributes very little sound in these circumstances. When the horn is played in a concert band it is better able to justify its existence in more than just a cosmetic way. However, it has to fight harder to be heard here than in a symphony orchestra, since it is surrounded by many forward-pointing instruments that can play much louder. There is consequently a temptation to try to compete with these more powerful instruments, a competition in which the horn is bound to lose. It is therefore necessary for the player to resign himself to being obscured, along with the bassoons, for much of the time and to be able to shine only occasionally.

Recording

Different problems arise when the horn player finds himself in the recording studio. The horn sound is one of the most difficult to reproduce, since it tends to sound too distant when picked up by the microphone. Inexperienced sound engineers may try to counter this by placing a microphone behind the player in a direct line with the bell. This gives definition, but the sound is not that of a horn. Another solution is to place screens behind the bells of the instruments to reflect the sound forward, but this also distorts the horn sound, making it hard and lacking in warmth. In the concert hall the listener is accustomed to the non-directional, warm sound of the horn, but this is extremely difficult to capture with a microphone without losing presence and clarity. It is regrettable that so many sound engineers are content with a distorted horn sound. This is most depressing and confusing for the player, who may be trying on the one hand to contend with a difficult, unflattering acoustic and on the other to compensate for the distorted sound being recorded, but the sensitive sound engineer is able to use his equipment to give the horn player clarity without losing the roundness of the sound.

Studio musicians

Many of the finest musicians play exclusively in the less secure but potentially more lucrative commercial world as session or studio musicians. In the commercial studio the horn player will find himself in a totally different environment from the concert hall or symphonic recording studio. Pop music is often recorded with each section, and sometimes each player, on a separate track, so that the engineer can achieve separation – that is to say, no overlap from one track to another. The instrumentalists are placed in separate booths and may not have any aural contact with each other, the ensemble being controlled by a central electronic metronome or 'click track' which is played over earphones. Many instruments are relatively unaffected by the lack of resonance in the studio but the inevitable close miking can totally destroy the horn sound.

From time to time it is physically impossible to get the musicians together at the same time and different tracks may be recorded at different times – occasionally in a different studio or even a different country. When this happens the player must keep in touch with the music already recorded by listening to the tape with the aid of earphones. This poses another problem, because if both ears are covered the player does not hear his own playing. The studio musician must above all be adaptable. He must be able to sight read and to play in many styles from 'straight' to jazz. His life is a lot different from the more orderly place in a symphony orchestra, where the schedules are arranged, but many players prefer the independence and the exposure to so many different types of music.

Chamber music

There are only two major works in the chamber music literature that feature the horn. The Mozart Quintet for Horns and Strings (K 407), which is actually more difficult than any of Mozart's four concertos, is a delight to play, a favourite with horn players and public alike.

The Brahms Trio was written with the hand horn in mind, and there are several passages in the work which, even if they are only harmonies, would benefit from being played with the hand. The veiled sound that the horn makes when half stopped would have been in Brahms's mind when he wrote these passages. Of course a performance using a hand horn would have to be balanced by using a piano from Brahms's time, as the modern super concert grand makes an altogether different sound.

The two big chamber music pieces that include winds are the Schubert Octet and the Beethoven Septet; although they are wonderful pieces to play, the horn parts are, in the soloistic sense, only of secondary importance to the clarinet. Nevertheless the horn has an important role to play, as in this solo from the Beethoven Septet:

A player can get a great deal of gratification from making a sound that blends with the clarinet and bassoon in such passages as this, from the same work:

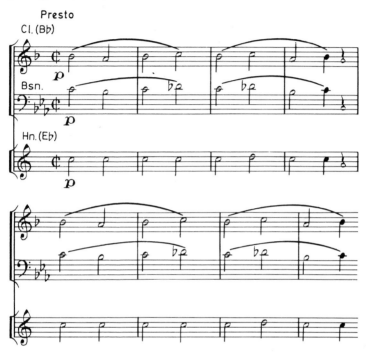

Apart from these works, the horn has more to play in the wind quintet repertoire, which is as near as the winds can get to a stable ensemble like the string quartet. Carl Nielsen wrote the one major romantic quintet which is both satisfying for the player and the listener. The long duet with the bassoon is particularly gratifying from the player's point of view:

Horn

But there are many occasions in the Nielsen quintet when
the horn must sublimate any soloistic tendencies and blend
into the wind choir, as in:

However, the horn is given a variation entirely to itself.

Nielsen wrote this quintet for five of his friends and the characters of the players are depicted musically in the different sections of the last movement. In this horn variation, the player has a wonderful opportunity to re-interpret the composer's wishes.

187

Horn

Most of the other quintets, particularly those by Reicha and Danzi, have conventional horn parts. But the Schoenberg remains one of the most challenging of all. The horn part is extremely tiring, because of the amount of playing required and the enormous jumps from register to register, as in the examples on p. 154. There are some passages in which the player would like to show off his technical prowess, but which must be frustratingly kept in the background. Here is an example:

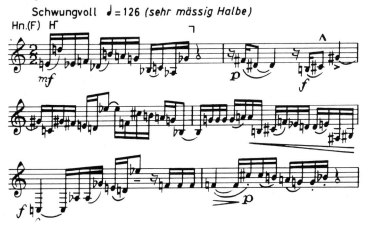

For all its reputation as a cold, clinical twelve-tone exercise, this quintet is potentially a highly romantic piece. Take for instance the opening of the slow movement:

Solo playing

Solo playing is the goal of most players, although few since the eighteenth century have been able to move very far from the orchestra. Psychologically there is a great difference between playing orchestral solos and being the soloist in a concerto. Even with the most indulgent of conductors, the orchestral solo must be part of another person's overall concept, and the orchestral player may feel somewhat lost when he has all the responsibilities of an interpretation to himself.

It feels different, too, to be playing in front of the orchestra rather than from within and the player can experience something of a shock, for instance, to find himself so close to the conductor. Then there is the close proximity of the audience, which is usually a long way from the player and is now at his feet. Apart from these visual images there is the acoustical difference. The horn player is more used to hearing the orchestra in front of him and of course now the sound is behind him. His own sound will be different and there may be a feeling of a lack of projection. If the horn soloist chooses to play seated, he has a double disadvantage. Visually he will appear to be a *tutti* player and his sound will tend to be absorbed by the string players who surround him, whereas if he stands up the listener will be reassured and feel that he is being given a performance. The soloist's sound will be above the front desks of strings and he will be able to project his interpretation in a way that will be of greater service to the composer.

A soloist must re-evaluate his conception of dynamics and must adopt a new musical approach, for now he is leading not only the conductor but the entire orchestra.

Nervous tension is a problem that confronts every performer, and although it may not be entirely eliminated, it can be controlled. Any task that entails risk will cause the person involved at least some apprehension, and if the player is ready to extend himself to the very limits, as he must in every good performance, there will always be an element of risk. The only means of control is to recognize the symptoms as soon as they appear, which may be hours before the event. It is then a matter of mentally keeping ahead and being able to concentrate on the technical and physical routine of playing. This concentration must however be based on reliable knowledge acquired during practice and performance in the past. If technique has been acquired without thought and is left to instinct, the task of controlling nerves may be too big. It is therefore imperative for the student to learn as soon as possible exactly how he plays his instrument. Only thus will he be able to contain his panic and apply himself to his playing.

The soloist's repertoire. It is common for the concert-goer to assume that the horn has only a limited solo repertoire. This is actually not so at all, particularly in the concerto repertoire. The 'bread and butter' concertos are, of course, the four by Mozart and the two by Richard Strauss. There are as well two by Joseph Hadyn and a concertino by his brother Michael, a concertino by Weber and a charming short concerto by Telemann. Then there are literally dozens written by lesser known composers; six survive from the original fourteen or fifteen by Giovanni Punto, over twenty by Rosetti (alias Rösler) and a couple by Christoph Foerster. There was a regrettable dearth of concertos in the nineteenth century and apart from the Richard Strauss No. 1 none of any significance was written until he wrote his second concerto. After this, there is a sadly neglected one by Hindemith. Composers in Britain, where there has been a tradition of solo horn playing, have produced a great many first-class concertos. No list is ever complete but the most popular ones are by Gordon Jacob, Don Banks, Malcolm Arnold, Iain Hamilton, Alun Hoddinott, Thea Musgrave, Richard Rodney Bennett, Elizabeth Lutyens and Robin Holloway. But perhaps the most famous work written in the twentieth century for solo horn is the Serenade for Tenor, Horn and Strings by Benjamin Britten.

The sounds of horn and piano are difficult to match. Nevertheless there are many fine works written both as sonatas for horn and for horn solo with piano accompaniment. The Beethoven sonata is one of the most popular with the public and is well within the range of all horn players. It was written for that most celebrated *corno secondo* Giovanni Punto, and although the horn does not have to play any high notes there are many awkward leaps and some very low notes, as in these extracts:

These low notes are what are called 'factitious' notes and do not exist in the harmonic series. It is possible with a strong embouchure to 'lip' the second harmonic downwards and, by closing the bell as much as possible with the right hand, to fake the note. The arpeggios at the end of the first and third movements are a hallmark of Punto's facile technique. Very difficult passages like these occur in all of Punto's own concertos and one can only assume that he excelled in them. It would therefore be logical for Beethoven, having heard Punto rattle off these astounding technical feats, to have written similar passages for him in this sonata.

A delightful but far less well-known sonata was composed by Franz Danzi, the Mannheim composer who wrote many symphonies and operas. He is remembered today mainly for his music for wind instruments, and he did indeed compose eight wind quintets as well as the two sonatas for horn and piano. The E♭ Sonata also bursts out from time to time in the Puntoesque way, as in this passage:

But it also contains some very jolly melodies, and it too uses the factitious tones referred to above:

There are many other works in the solo and chamber music repertoire that have not been examined. However the pieces chosen show the different styles of music and the various ways in which composers have written for the horn.

Eight
Teaching the Horn

Many players tire of the enormous strains put upon them in the orchestra and choose to take a teaching position and to play a little solo work and chamber music. This rather more secluded life in no way indicates a retirement; serious teaching is extremely strenuous, as no two students are alike and each requires a different approach. The different rate of progress of each student is something that is rarely catered for in teaching institutions and teachers must guard against forcing the slowest student beyond his physical ability, as the late developer can overtake the star virtuoso of the music academy.

It is often said that good players are often poor teachers, but it might be more accurate to say that bad players are *always* poor teachers. The only accurate test of a good teacher is the results he gets, but the experienced player must always have the advantage, having had the practical experience as a professional performer playing under performance conditions.

It is not really possible to teach the horn in the abstract. A teacher must have experienced a full professional life to be able to pass on the 'tricks of the trade', and it is fortunate that most of the leading players of the world also hold important teaching positions. A wind instrument teacher must be a diagnostician, as most of the physical activity of playing is internal, involving breathing and the use of the facial muscles. Consequently it is not possible to see exactly what the student is doing. Likewise, any demonstration by the teacher will only indicate things like posture and tone, the juxtaposition of breathing and muscle control being hidden from view.

It is not difficult to define what a trapeze artist must do in the physical sense, but it is an entirely different matter to put the description into practice, and although horn playing is not so potentially hazardous, it is in many ways as difficult to communicate the art of playing to the student.

It is obviously of prime importance for the teacher to communicate properly with the student. He must be able to demonstrate what he advocates, but it is very difficult to pick up technique by observation alone and there are many teachers who have only a sketchy idea of how they play, and with this incomplete knowledge they quite often give the student much highly inaccurate information. So it is up to the student to work at least as hard as his teacher and to contribute his own energies to the lessons. It is not sufficient for him to understand what the teacher says, he must also understand what is meant. So the student should never hesitate to ask sensible and pertinent questions that are relevant either to his lesson or to his own experiences during practice.

The student

The three actions that the student must co-ordinate are the forming of the lips into a position where they will vibrate (embouchure), the controlled exhalation of the breath from the lungs (breathing) and the minor interruption of this exhalation with the tongue (tonguing). The embouchure is a tricky subject on which to generalize and should ideally be left for the teacher and student to discuss.

The teacher must try to give the student a total realization of how he works physically and mentally and of how the instrument will react to different ways of making the air inside vibrate. The student has really to be taught how to teach himself during the 95 per cent of the time he is without an instructor. Every moment of playing must be used to experiment with technique so that, when he returns to his teacher for a lesson, he is able to show an improvement in his grasp of the complex art of horn playing.

Women horn players

It was once thought that, even if it were desirable for women to play wind instruments, they would not have sufficient stamina to compete with men, such arguments as smaller stature and limited lung capacity being put forward. In recent years it has been demonstrated that women are perfectly able to play the horn as well as men – in many cases better – and they are accepted more and more into positions of responsibility in orchestras. Any prejudice that survives is mostly against women as such, for it can no longer be said that they are not able to play as well as men.

Master classes

Master classes, sometimes referred to as 'clinics', are becoming more popular and attract many players and spectators. With this type of event it is not possible, nor is it desirable, to give the same sort of lesson that would be given on a one-to-one basis. The person giving the master class must be able to assess quickly the strengths and faults in the player's technique and musical approach and comment on these in a way that will be both of benefit to the player and of interest to the onlooker.

A player should never be ridiculed but should receive advice that will help him to perceive ways of improving his technique and style. Care must be taken not to quibble over aspects of playing that may have been taught in a different fashion; this is something to take up with the teacher. The master class may be the only time the player and instructor meet, so it is imperative that the student is given an overall perception of style and understands the physical approaches to playing. The student usually derives great benefit from this sort of public analysis of his playing by a person other than his regular teacher, and it frequently happens that a point that may have been made a hundred times before is grasped for the first time in public.

The serious student and the amateur musician

Finally it must be stressed that there are two categories of horn students, both relevant to this text. There is the so-called 'serious' student who hopes to play professionally and to teach. Then there is the amateur student whose only motivation is to enjoy himself. Both groups must be treated with respect, and it is the responsibility of the teacher to be able to predict into which category his student should go. It is irresponsible for a teacher to allow a student who will only ever be at best second-rate to waste valuable years and money training for a tough profession. Far better to face the facts early on and to aim for another position in music (administration, management, musicology, music teaching as a subject in itself); if the student has sufficient musical instinct but lacks the physical aptitude to play well, his training on the horn will not be wasted. But if he is a good musician and a potentially second-rate instrumentalist, he will have a miserable life. Playing the horn should never be a burden; it should be an inspiration and should be enjoyed.

There are some aspiring horn players who declare that they have no intention of playing in symphony orchestras. They are wrong! Apart from the sheer joy of playing the wonderful orchestral repertoire, both in the symphony and the opera orchestra – just think of the works of Wagner, Brahms, Mahler and Bruckner – there is the great opportunity to work with fine musicians. The horn is a passport to exciting musical experiences and in spite of the diversity of national styles there remains a close freemasonry amongst horn players, who, because they are aware of the difficulties of their art, have a deep mutual respect.

Above all there remains the special sound that the horn makes, which has been used by the greatest romantic composers. It is the players' privilege to interpret this music, and to uplift and inspire the listener. Horn playing is both a craft and an art, and although Bruno Jaenicke described the horn as 'the wild beast of the orchestra' it must also be remembered that Schumann called it 'the soul' of the orchestra.

Index

Index